Medium Memoirs

Messages of Love, Hope, and Reunion

Alaine Portner

BALBOA.
PRESS

A DIVISION OF HAY HOUSE

Balboa Press books may be ordered through booksellers or by contacting:

Balboa Press
A Division of Hay House
1663 Liberty Drive
Bloomington, IN 47403
www.balboapress.com
1 (877) 407-4847

Because of the dynamic nature of the Internet, any web addresses or links contained in this book may have changed since publication and may no longer be valid. The views expressed in this work are solely those of the author and do not necessarily reflect the views of the publisher, and the publisher hereby disclaims any responsibility for them.

The author of this book does not dispense medical advice or prescribe the use of any technique as a form of treatment for physical, emotional, or medical problems without the advice of a physician, either directly or indirectly. The intent of the author is only to offer information of a general nature to help you in your quest for emotional and spiritual well-being. In the event you use any of the information in this book for yourself, which is your constitutional right, the author and the publisher assume no responsibility for your actions.

Any people depicted in stock imagery provided by Thinkstock are models, and such images are being used for illustrative purposes only.
Certain stock imagery © Thinkstock.

Printed in the United States of America.

ISBN: 978-1-4525-8779-0 (sc)
ISBN: 978-1-4525-8780-6 (e)

Library of Congress Control Number: 2013921759

Balboa Press rev. date: 12/20/2013

Contents

A Note to the Reader...

This book is the result of the collaborative effort of friends, family members, clients of the Yoga Center of Medford, and our dearly departed. We have shared these stories of spiritual communication in the hope that you, the reader, will receive them as the generous gifts they are, and allow them to transform any fears you harbor about the afterlife. As you'll see in these pages, your loved ones are always just a breath away.

The dialogue in each story is unique, sometimes cumulative, and always subject to the recipient's readiness. No communication from spirit is ever the same. During these dates with divine energy, the beliefs of many sitters about Heaven, Earth, life, and death, were radically transformed. Through their gifts of trust, they received that most precious of treasures: hope.

The people who contributed their stories to this book have not received any pay or recognition for their participation (except maybe some good karma). Rather, they chose to share their stories in the hope that you will open your heart and mind to the possibility of life beyond death, and learn to trust what you sense with regard to the infinite. In order to protect the privacy of these generous souls, many names have been changed; the accounts of their readings have also been edited for length, clarity, and flow.

So let's begin, before it all ends...

Preface

On the early morning hours of September 9, 2001, I woke from a terrible nightmare that I didn't understand.

In my dream, I'd seen two unfamiliar towers bisected by two airplanes. It was a terrifying image for which I had no rational explanation, and it rocked my balance and focus.

At the time, I was busy opening my new yoga center in Medford, New Jersey, totally preoccupied with building permits and real estate transactions. After nine long and frustrating months, I'd started trying to psychically pick up on the dates when all of these transactions would settle. I was already interested in the universal telepathic component of the human emotional bandwidth—and if I could get some answers about my own project, so much the better. I also knew that dreams are often messages from Spirit. However, the chance that I might have a nightmare of epic proportions had never entered my consciousness.

I shared the strange dream with a few people, trying to understand what it might mean, but everyone was as confused as I was. Then, on September 11, we all received the wake-up call of a lifetime. We woke to a new worldview of terrorism and destruction—but also to our country's patriotism, unity, and heroism in the face of tragic loss.

And in the midst of it all, I was catapulted into a greater understanding of my personal purpose on this planet.

Living in New Jersey, so close to Ground Zero, our community felt the full impact of this unprecedented sequence of events. We knew that many beautiful souls had sacrificed their earthly existence to bring more love and light to this planet, so we set about creating a labyrinth of light in their honor. Within two days, the Yoga Center became a safe haven for all those seeking solace and a quiet place to pray as they searched for answers to this unspeakable tragedy. We held prayer and meditation sessions, community gatherings, and healing workshops.

My own jolt into psychic awareness frightened me greatly. For nearly two years after my dream, I drew my psychic senses inward and went into a sort of energetic hibernation. But gradually, as our Center grew and the initial shock of 9/11 dissipated, I began to soften back into the connection which had always served me so well. I asked

Spirit how I could use this connection to serve my friends and family, visitors to the center, and those who had departed this earthly life.

It was at this point that my gift of psychic mediumship fully revealed itself. By tapping into the vast reservoir of energy that is Spirit, I can reunite people with loved ones who have crossed to the other side, and communicate messages from those who no longer have earthly voices with which to speak.

My personal style of channeling offers news you can use today— but the practice of conversing with spirits isn't a new reality show: in fact, it's as old as the human race. Our ancestors had a much deeper and more defined connection to the spirit realms than most of us enjoy today. All cultures have historically prayed to "sources" greater than themselves: gurus, saints, gods, avatars, or ancestors. Sometimes, this communication could take the form of a nearly continuous dialogue. Sometimes, it showed up as channeled writings—like the Bible, or the Upanishads. And sometimes, it came as a brief glimpse into a world beyond what the five senses can perceive; a momentary glimpse of a spirit, or a whisper on the wind. However messages from Spirit show up in our lives, their underlying universal messages of peace have the power to speak to all of us.

There is a profound richness of guidance and support around each and every one of us; it begs us to open our hearts to all living energies. "In-spirit-ation" abounds! The departed speak through me, but their messages aren't filled with fear. In fact, these spirits speak of how we might live more lovingly and compassionately, without fear, loss, or sorrow.

I am a yoga and meditation teacher, but you don't have to practice yoga to benefit from the teachings in this book. The yogic path can be rich in joy and health, but being able to stand on your head or twist yourself into a pretzel isn't a prerequisite for expanding your consciousness into the realm of Spirit. All you need is curiosity and an open mind. On this planet, we are all students seeking knowledge, balance, and connection with the universal consciousness, but the paths we walk in pursuit of that knowledge are as individual as we are. It is my intention that the words on these pages grant you insight, and empower your personal journey.

CHANNEL 1

Transformations

Those you love are always with you, even when you can't see them.

The boundary between the two worlds we call Heaven and Earth isn't fixed; it's flexible. Our five senses don't always allow us to perceive the spiritual realm, but that doesn't mean that those who reside there don't touch our lives and penetrate our perceptive barriers. Sometimes, they're content to allow us to feel their presence in a gust of wind that ruffles our hair, or in the way their favorite songs, images, or symbols quite literally jump out at us. At other times, they come to us with more specific messages which can help us move through difficult times with lighter hearts.

That's where I come in.

My psychic jump-start on September 9, 2001 expanded my bandwidth and confirmed that I could access information from other locations and destinations. Although it took me a while to get comfortable with this new and unique ability, once I chose to direct it in service to my community, I started to sense the presence of spirits all around me. They appeared in yoga classes, meditation sessions, even on family outings.

At first, this was rather alarming: I mean, how do you explain to your family and friends that you've suddenly developed a knack for talking to transitioned souls? But gradually, I began to see that my gift was just that: a gift. Spirits reach out to me because I am a channel for their voices. I amplify their messages and intentions so that their loved ones can hear them loud and clear. By employing my psychic talents in service to the loved ones of these spirits who came to call, I can facilitate purposeful guidance and transformation in many lives.

I've received thousands of spirit communications over the years. A good portion of these were from spirits who wished for their loved ones to move out of the debilitating and contracted state of mourning. When someone we love passes over, it's natural to feel grief and pain, both for the departed and for our own suffering at their loss. Much of this grief stems from the belief that we are separated from our loved one, that we will never again hear their voices or receive their words of wisdom—but Heaven isn't a remote location. Once we are given proof that our loved ones are still here, watching over us, that grief can be eased and even transformed.

That's exactly what happened when David introduced himself to me.

David: the Angel of Love (and Technology)

I have a playful, charming group of girlfriends with whom I train for 5Ks, marathons, and triathlons. Our kids are all about the same age, and we shared a lot of laughter and tears during those aptly titled "formative years." There are six of us, and after we'd finished passing around a dog-eared copy of *The Sisterhood of the Traveling Pants*, we started calling ourselves the "Ya-Yas."

As the kids got older and life got busier, we started seeing less of one another. Missy moved to Connecticut, while Judy bravely stepped into life as a newly single mother of three. I was busy with the Yoga Center, trying to balance business ownership with yoga practice and my newfound calling to channel.

In 2010, I invited the Ya-Yas to spend a weekend at my family's house at the Jersey Shore. It had been far too long since we'd had a Sisterhood party, and I was feeling the need to connect with my girls over more than just a marathon. When at last we were gathered in the living room before a roaring fire, I couldn't stop grinning.

Over platters of finger food, we took turns catching the others up on our lives. However, when it was my turn to talk, I found myself holding back. Since the last time we'd all been together, my perspective on how the world works had shifted drastically. It wasn't just that I was seeing spirits; I was re-working my entire spiritual belief system! I discovered that I wasn't comfortable sharing some of the more extreme ideas that were rolling around in my consciousness, because I wasn't sure that they would be accepted or understood, even by my dearest friends. What would my Ya-Yas think if I told them I could talk to spirits? Would they laugh, and tell me I'd finally done a header off the deep end? Would they go all cold and silent, and pretend I'd never broached the subject? I didn't feel brave enough to find out. So I breezed through some fluffy news about my kids and the Yoga Center, and passed the baton to Judy.

Suddenly, there was a deafening clatter from the kitchen. We all jumped.

"What the heck was that?" Erin hissed.

The noises continued. Pots and pans rattled. Doors opened and slammed shut. Utensils jangled in their drawers. The Ya-Yas exchanged nervous looks. I shrugged apologetically. Although I was beginning to understand what was happening, I still wasn't ready to come out of the closet. I just stood there, feeling more and more uncomfortable, as the clamor escalated.

Finally, there came a gigantic *crash*. We all screamed. I ran to the kitchen to discover that a whole shelf full of pots and pans had been pulled right off the wall!

Obviously, someone really, really wanted our attention. And that someone wasn't going to stop tearing my kitchen to pieces until I stepped up and used my gift to orchestrate communication.

I took a deep breath, and marched back into the living room to face my shaking friends. "Do any of you know of a recently deceased spirit who might want to connect with you?"

"What?"

"What are you talking about?"

"Alaine, are you saying there's a *ghost* in your kitchen?" That one brought on some giggles—from everyone except Judy, who looked thoughtful.

I tried not to wince. "Not a ghost: a *spirit*. He feels like someone young, with a connection to cooking and the Jersey Shore."

"Oh, my God," Judy whispered. "It could be my nephew, David, who passed away from a brain tumor just a few months ago. He loved to cook. One of the last times I saw him was here in Ocean City! That was when he was still healthy."

Judy had shared this intense story with the Ya-Yas near the time that David passed. I remembered how heartbroken both Judy and David's parents had been when he transitioned to the other side. "He has something to say to you," I told her. "Would you like to hear from him?"

Judy's big blue eyes filled with tears as she nodded. "I've been praying for a sign that he's okay."

I sensed that it wasn't the right time for a session—everyone was still too jumpy—so I made an appointment with David's spirit for the following morning. After that, things quieted down in the kitchen, but the comfortable, relaxed atmosphere had been shattered. I explained a bit about the channeling process to the Ya-Yas to calm their fears and pique their interest (after all, I was the "ghost host" in the house!), and told them that prior experience assured me that this communication would be positive and heart-warming, not scary at all. Then, I wished them all sweet dreams, and went to bed.

That night, I barely slept. I wasn't nervous because my gift had finally been revealed to the Ya-Yas—that part had gone fairly well, considering the circumstances—but because I was going to be channeling a young person's spirit. The death of a child is always terribly tragic, and channeling such a spirit can feel invasive to grieving loved ones if they're not ready to hear what's being said. I wondered if David's strong presence was forcing a reading on Judy even though she might not be ready for it.

As it turned out, I needn't have worried. The appearance of a spirit to his or her loved ones always occurs in divine timing. As we arranged ourselves in a circle in the living room the next morning, the sun streamed through the windows, warming our shoulders gently. Judy looked nervous, but she was smiling. Nina was intrigued and excited, and asked if my style was similar to what she had seen on television and in the movies.

"This isn't my show," I said, as I settled in to my seat. "It's not about me, it's about the message. But given this spirit's volume in the kitchen last night, I suggest you put your seat belts on!"

"Is he here?" Judy asked. "Is David here?"

I took a deep breath, and invited David's presence to emerge. Immediately, I was filled with a sense of courage, intelligence, and security. "Yes, he's here," I said. "He feels so young and light. He's good-looking, smart, and strong. When spirits show up as their best selves, it tells me that they're at peace, and beyond any dis-ease. I can definitely say from this first impression that David is in a better place."

During the first part of any channeling session, I spend a lot of time listening and taking notes. Spirits don't step into my body, like they did to Whoopi Goldberg in the movie *Ghost*. Instead, they pass me words, images, feelings, and sometimes even smells. I translate these things onto the page so I can speak about them more clearly with the recipient.

The Ya-Yas fidgeted as my pen flew across the notebook pages. Finally, when the download was complete, I spoke again, using the words that David prompted me to say. "Pardon the intrusion, Aunt Judy. I want to reach out. I want to talk about my light body because my parents are so heavy. If they knew or felt my relief, it would ease their burden."

I blinked, and asked, "Does he really talk like that?" It seemed a little out of character for a man who'd been only twenty-six when he died. But Judy nodded. "That sounds like him. He was very intelligent."

I asked David for additional confirmation. He instructed me to mention pants with a zipper. At that point, Judy began to cry.

"Oh my God! It's really him!"

I often receive signs from spirits that I don't understand, but which immediately resonate with the receiver. This was obviously one of them.

I moved on to the next part of David's transmission. "When we understand we can live strong like Armstrong, especially with more fund-raising research, we don't need to mourn our losses. It was my destiny to leave this world young. It's wild to intellectually see from this side of Heaven!"

"We're creating a 'Live Strong' benefit in David's name, to raise money for research," Judy explained to the Ya-Yas.

"He showed me a symbol," I continued. "It's a V with a downward-facing 3 on top of it to make a heart. Do the 3 and the V have any significance to you?"

"He used to make hearts like that in e-mail and texts," Jules confirmed. "He was very tech-savvy. Also, our family name begins with 'V.'"

"I'm getting the sense that he wants this to be a logo of some sort."

"We were looking for a T-shirt design for the fundraiser. Maybe he wants us to use that one!"

I shared more of the words I'd received from David. "Thank you for returning to Ocean City and for bringing a friend who could relay my message. Aunt Judy, the reason I was able to find you is because I knew you would listen. You felt my spirit through the loud mixing bowls because I can mix recipes of realities. It is nothing to be scared about, because we can all feel each other whenever we desire. When we are mourning it pulls us away from possibility, and we live more densely in our bodies. It was adventurous to shed my body during transition. My dad needs to shed his: he built a wall around his heart while caring for me. My father wanted to switch places with me. I can't feel pain or sorrow here, but I can see it all around my family. So is it possible, Judy, for you to reach out to my mom? I'm in a different residential place in Heaven for having passed so young, but I'm here with my grandfather, 'B.' There is a long history up here, and not the kind of history I studied in college! Mine was an early calling, but it had more to do with my parents' life experience than my own passing. I knew this long before they were willing to accept my departure."

Judy affirmed this. "He knew he was dying. He told his parents he loved them, and not to worry, and then he put himself to bed. He passed away a few hours later."

A few more things were shared: the fact that David's godchild, Judy's nephew, often reached out to him for guidance; a crystal on a windowsill; the way he used to leave his cereal bowl out on the kitchen counter all the time. "Tell Dad to remember Captain Crunch," he asked me to say. "Tell him to be his own captain, and champion himself out of his grief while he is still on Earth."

Finally, David said, "Judy, you are open-minded and full of love without too much fear. This is how I found you and you found me."

He waved, and a wave of emotion swept through the room. "You're waiting for your own wave to come in. Thank you for teaching others to trust in the spiritual world, without fear of the future. Love me always, I love you!"

And with that, he was gone.

All of the Ya-Yas fell to the floor in exhaustion. I found myself crying just as hard as the others. We didn't speak, just hugged and wept and laughed and hugged some more. All around us, we could feel David's angelic presence. It was a miraculous, intimate experience, beyond the scope of words.

Later, Judy explained more of what had been said. We were all curious about the mention of the zipper as confirmation of David's identity. Judy shared with us that as his tumor got worse, David started losing the ability to perform small motor tasks. On one really bad day, he spent an hour struggling with the zipper on his pants. He solved the problem by wearing the same sweatpants every day thereafter. The crystal on the windowsill had been a gift; he was fascinated by the way the refracted light spilled over the walls of his room. His cereal bowl became a kitchen counter centerpiece, a reminder of how he created playful recipes with all food groups, including cereal. Toward the end of his earthly life, he stopped using the cereal bowl; his hands were unsteady, and he was afraid he would break it.

As more and more details were confirmed by Judy, a sense of awe stole over the Ya-Yas. The enormity of what we had witnessed kept us in a joyful daze for the rest of the day. Our group's bond was reaffirmed and sealed in support of Judy's loss, and we basked in a deepened sense of sisterhood.

*   *   *

The recognition that Heaven and Earth exist simultaneously and within reach of one another can lift enormous amounts of emotional weight from our shoulders. Judy was so relieved by the confirmation of David's well-being that she wanted to share the news with her sister and brother-in-law as soon as possible. She also suggested that they contact me for a reading as soon as they felt ready.

I wasn't sure that I had the courage to channel a child's spirit to his bereaved parents, but I had to trust that nothing would happen until the time was right.

David's spirit stayed with me for days after I channeled him. He was so sweet, and (as Judy had confirmed) very tech-savvy. He assisted me with many mechanical complications, like setting up software on my computer. When his parents reached out to say they were ready for a session, he urged me to set up our session through Skype. As I didn't have that program, we used Judy's laptop—which, coincidentally, David had set up for her when he was still healthy.

David let me know that he wanted to schedule the session on "V-day," Valentine's Day. Judy was on hand to act as a witness to this first post-passing communication.

David's parents had not entered his bedroom since his death— but on V-day, they opened that door for the first time. When their expectant, nervous faces appeared on my computer screen, I could see that they were sitting on the edge of David's bed. Their choice of seat felt symbolic to me, as I was also at the edge of my professional comfort zone.

Immediately, I felt David's light presence, and all of my nervousness dissolved. In addition to the words he wanted me to share; I was given a visual of the word USHER, broken into pieces: US-SHE-HE-R. US, for his family. SHE, for his mother. HE for his father. R for "Are." It was David's way of telling me that he still considered himself an integral part of his family, even though he wasn't physically present.

Again, he asked everyone's pardon for his intrusion. "I'm doing more on the other side than I did when I was here," he said through me. "Or at least, more than I did in that last year! My brain isn't working overtime here. I'm tapping into euphoria: this place is for *me*."

He showed me the heart and number 3 again, as confirmation of his family name and his favorite tech sentiment. "Thank you for connecting on a Hallmark holiday. Valentine's Day can 'mark' our communication in the 'halls' of Spirit. There really are halls here, and different sections for every imaginable learning process!"

I got the impression that he liked the word "current," because it can apply to a current of energy, or a 'current' time. I shared this with his parents before speaking David's words. "I am speaking to you 'currently.' This allows you to open your heart instead of protecting it against my loss. You did not lose me; I'm just not physically visible! I like being a conduit. You can be a Land Mind, and I can support you until we are together again. Broaden your perspective of time, location and life. Our love is just as thick in its measurements."

He showed me the V and 3 again. "Someone is thinking of this design. You can decide if this is a heart which is broken, or just separated. Don't do this fundraiser for me; do it instead because it makes you feel better."

David's mother, Eileen, nodded tensely. I could tell that she still didn't believe in this process one hundred percent. David's father, Dave, sat motionless.

"Thank you for all you provided for me," David continued. "It's okay to change my room, Mom. Except for a few keepsakes, everything should be put to rest. I have no more need for my clothes: you know it was only sweatpants for me! If you want me to be in the house with you, I will—but I don't need the anchors of heavy hearts and old outfits to keep me there. I know this is harder for you than for me, but I AM NOT SUFFERING. Are you suffering?"

David's parents were still very subdued. It was almost like what I was conveying was not quite real to them. I felt pushed by David to ask, "There's something purple—seriously purple—that's a reference to love. Is it there in the bedroom?"

"It's a picture from his prom," Eileen told me. "His date is wearing a very, *very* purple dress."

The picture wasn't something I, or even Judy, could had known about before this reading. Both Eileen and the elder David seemed to soften a little in their resistance.

David mentioned his love of the ocean and nature, and that he was sharing space in Heaven with his grandfather, "B," and another female relative, "S." "It's good to have the male-female balance," he said, "Just like at home. But you two should *leave* home—a trip to Europe? Cruising?"

Eileen gasped. Tears streamed down her cheeks. Dave explained, "I just got a call yesterday from our travel agent. Two spots on a European cruise just opened up. I wasn't sure if we should go. We really haven't left the house much since David passed away, and we didn't tell anyone we were thinking about traveling."

"Not even me!" Judy interjected with a smile.

"Say yes to the trip," David told them. "Have a joyful adventure with my blessing."

As I conveyed his next words, I felt lightness spread through me. "My request is that you have lighter hearts. There is deep compassion for you from family, friends, and neighbors, but the fact is, my completion of this life cycle won't change, so *you* have to change. Consider this my scientific experiment in love. I am engineering from above. Please open your hearts and minds to the experiments of eternal love."

He also asked me to convey his love to his sister's son. "He has changed because of my transition, but he is full of determination. He speaks to me often."

When the session came to a close, David shared these final words with his parents. "Love to all. David I am, David I was. Thank you for allowing me to be in your hearts in a different way. I am cared for and surrounded by love and peace. I love you, Mom and Dad!"

He signed off with a V and 3, which we all now knew was his symbol for an open heart.

*   *   *

David's reunion with his parents remains one of the most beautiful and powerful communications I have ever channeled. His spirit was so light and loving; truly, he is an archangel in the making!

He appeared to me several more times over the months following the session with his parents. He became my "technology angel." Whenever I was having computer issues, I would send out a prayer to David, and soon the situation would be resolved. He also shared his wisdom in other ways, and urged me to be professionally available for grieving families, whichever side of the veil they were on.

Nearly a year after our Valentine's Day session, I received a letter from David's parents. A portion of it is printed here.

Dear Alaine,

Judy has been after us for months to write to you about the cruise we took in October, after you mentioned that our son David wanted us to "Say yes to the trip." We had a wonderful time on the trip with our old friends, and met many new ones.

There were two things about the trip that which made us really believe that David wanted us to go.

First, while we were waiting for our flight in the Atlanta airport, we met a couple from Jacksonville who lost a daughter to brain cancer six years ago. We were the first people they had ever met who had also lost a child to this disease. We became fast friends and ended up spending most of the trip with them. There was a lot of storytelling, reminiscing, tears, and laughter. It was a comfort to all of us to know that others had lived through this experience.

Then, one day, we sat next to a different couple at lunch. After we introduced ourselves, we discovered that they were from San Diego, and that the husband was a neurosurgeon. As it turned out, his former partner was the doctor who'd performed the brain biopsy on our son David! (I'm getting the chills just typing this!) We spoke a bit about David's case. He told us that his partner was an excellent surgeon, and offered to introduce us to him. The introduction took place during the exact week that David's biopsy had been performed the previous year.

I don't know if these new friendships were why David wanted us to take that cruise, but we offer our sincere thanks for letting David's spirit contact us through you. As much as we doubted the possibility of his communicating with us, we are now convinced that it can occur. Although our sense of loss is still great, the messages you conveyed have comforted us in many ways. Thank you for sharing your gift with us.

Eileen & Dave

Irene's Latest Appointment

Spirits can give us a glimpse into what happens after we die, but they can also offer angelic advice about how to live. Souls who have passed still want to interact with the ones they love, just as their loved ones want to interact with them. The resulting alchemy of loving communication can be transformative for everyone involved.

Tina contacted me for a reading during the Christmas holiday season. She and her father Charlie were hoping to connect with her mother Irene, who had recently transitioned to the other side. I totally understood their desire: the first holiday without a loved one can be traumatic. While everyone else is caught up in the traditional Christmas frenzy, the bereaved can feel motionless, sad, and unanchored. It's hard to make new and happy memories when someone dear is missing. The pain of their loss had driven Tina and Charlie apart: they had barely spoken since Irene's passing. The fact that they were coming together for this session was incredible, and told me that they were both ready to receive some healing.

As soon as I invited Irene's spirit to open to me, I felt an agonizing pain in my stomach. It felt like bile was flowing up into my lungs. I tried to breathe more deeply to ease the pain, but that only made it worse. Tina watched me with concern as I struggled to blurt, "Please tell me that Irene died of a stomach issue!"

I felt an immediate constriction, and then the pain receded like a wave pulling away from shore. Holding back tears, Tina and Charlie confirmed that Irene had indeed died as a result of severe abdominal complications.

Irene spoke through me, loud and clear. "There's a bubble between you two. You used to be so close, but this grief is pushing you apart. It's like an emotional pressure bubble. You are here for a reunion. I've been waiting for this appointment. I hope that our time together reduces the mourning process which is so evident to me."

Father and daughter smiled together. "Everything she did was an 'appointment,'" Charlie explained to me. "She would even have called this session an appointment. It was her way of dealing with the constant doctors' visits. I'm *still* canceling appointments that we made before her death."

I asked, "Why does she appear in so much white? It's all around her. It suits her presence because she's so peaceful."

"She loved to wear white," Tina replied. "In one of our favorite pictures of her, she's wearing an all-white outfit."

"I was thinking of that same picture," Charlie said.

"She is very expressive," I told them. "Was there something remarkable about her appearance at the time of her dying?"

Charlie proceeded to share with me how he found his wife's body. She had to make frequent pit stops because of her terrible acid reflux. He would always go into the bathroom with her to make sure that she was okay—but this one time he waited outside in the car while she used the bathroom at their son's house. When she didn't come out after several minutes, he dashed in to find her dead on the bathroom floor. "If I had gone in with her, maybe I could have done something," he said. "I think about that moment every day. But the expression on her face was so peaceful!"

Irene asked me to say, "That's because I didn't feel the pain while I was transitioning. I saw the Pearly Gates opening for me, and knew everything was going to be okay."

Both father and daughter recognized these as Irene's words. She often spoke about the Pearly Gates of Heaven during her life; they were a symbol of her Catholic faith.

Next, Irene showed me a piece of pearl jewelry. She asked me to tell Tina to change the setting and wear it often as a reminder. Tina laughed. "I have a black pearl ring that was my mom's," she told me. "I talked to a jeweler about changing the setting earlier this week."

"There's a lot of energy around the word 'union,'" I said. "There are many significant associations there."

"Yes," Charlie confirmed. "We live on Union Street. And her father was very active in the Teamsters Union."

"This meeting is a new 'union' for our family," Irene said through me. "You both have been breathing very shallowly. You need to monitor the air quality around you."

"Mom was always concerned about air pollution," Tina explained. "Her father died of asbestos poisoning, and her mother was a chain smoker. She was always telling us to take care of ourselves and breathe."

"Give yourselves time to heal in this separation," Irene continued. "You only have to do this on Earth. In Heaven, there are no feelings but love. Oh, and Charles, no regrets about not finding me sooner. My death was mine, not yours. We each have our own exit, so how can you be responsible for mine? You found me because you wouldn't have trusted anyone else's story if they found me first. You have always shown your love by being there for our family. Sweep that guilt outside, NOW! Please!"

As I conveyed this message, I could see the weight lifting off of Charlie's shoulders. He wept for a long time, finally released from the guilt he'd been holding for many months.

We were quiet for a while. Then, Irene prompted me to say, "Oh, and Charles? Go and get a new TV!"

That made him laugh aloud. "The darned thing just broke last week!"

After a few final words of love, Irene stepped aside to make room for the spirit of Carlo, Charlie's father. I translated his character as a policeman, always showing up for others as a knight in shining armor. I felt that he, like Irene, had suffered from stomach and heart issues. "He is very round," I said. "And he loves Frank Sinatra! I get a vision of him standing on a Philadelphia street corner with his buddies, singing Sinatra's tunes *a cappella.*"

"He did love Frank Sinatra," Charlie reminisced.

"There's also a sense of responsibility. He wants me to say that you are not in complete control of love, time, money, or circumstances, or even food."

Then, Carlo prompted me to shout, "Ice cream!"

Tina giggled. "He used to say to us, 'You can't have ice cream if you eat the crabs!' It was his way of keeping the kids away from the crabs at our family cookouts. He wanted more for himself!"

Charlie started laughing, too, so hard that his whole body shook. When the moment had passed, he looked fondly at his daughter and said, "I don't think I've laughed like that since your mother passed away."

Tina took his hand, and my eyes filled with tears. I could feel Irene beaming at her husband and daughter, thrilled that she had been able to be a part of this reunion. Next to her, Carlo's spirit exuded self-satisfaction; he loved to make his son laugh.

*   *   *

What I've learned from spirits like Irene is that love is eternal. In Heaven, it translates into a "knowing energetic faith" which is powerful and enduring. The bonds of family remain, but they're both strengthened and diffused. In my psychic sight, this energy shows up like a glittering rainbow.

I certainly saw the rainbow around Charlie and Tina that day. Irene might be showing up for them in a new and different way, but Mom is still taking care of her family—and, as usual, she arrives for all of her appointments in perfect time.

Butterfly Kisses

One of the most romantic reconnections I've experienced happened between Lynn, a student at the Yoga Center, and her recently departed husband, Maurice.

The first time Maurice showed up wasn't during a channeling session, but during a Pilates class. I couldn't identify him, but I sensed his spirit floating around Lynn. When class was over, I pulled her aside and asked if she would be willing to attend a group spirit meditation session, as there was someone who wanted to contact her. She readily agreed.

Maurice was so full of love for his wife that I felt like I would burst just trying to express it. There weren't enough words to contain what he wanted to say. What came through was, "Lynn, I see you in your mirror every morning. You are so beautiful. I know that you are thinking of me at those times. I hear your loving thoughts when you are holding your deep purple velvet pillow. I am still here, and I love you."

Lynn confirmed that she did, indeed, sleep curled around a deep purple pillow, cuddling up to it in her loneliness. I could tell that she was a little shocked by the strength of Maurice's presence, but also that she was comforted to know that her beloved was still with her every morning.

"I'm trying to make some big choices right now," Lynn told the group. "I have to decide how to care for my son, who really misses his dad. I have to decide whether to sell the house we've lived in for years. It's so hard! I keep wishing he was still around to help me figure out what to do!"

"You won't make the wrong decision," Maurice prompted me to say. "I'm still here to oversee even the smallest decisions—but whatever you choose to do, there is no judgment, so carry on fully." Then, he showed me a vision of Lynn in a black cocktail dress. "You need to buy the tight-fitting black dress for our daughter's wedding. You look great in it!"

"Oh, crap!" Lynn screamed. "He was watching me in the dressing room! That's hysterical! I've been trying to decide whether it is appropriate to wear black as the mother of the bride. I don't want to look like a widow."

"I will be there at the wedding," Maurice assured his wife. "Somehow, you'll know I'm there."

After that session, Lynn wrote to me.

Dear Alaine,

You have given me a wonderful gift from the man I love. Maurice was my everything. Losing him has sent me through every emotion in the book—but now I know, deep down inside, even during my lowest of lows, that he was and is with me.

The comfort I received from our meditation session has been greater than any therapy. Going to that Pilates class in January was purely spontaneous, yet in my heart, I know it was meant to be.

I have wanted to see, hear, and feel Maurice beside me. I never had a lot of confidence in myself, and after I lost him I lost even more. I would cry on that purple pillow that you mentioned and yearn for him to come back to me, to love and protect me. Often, I thought I felt him nearby, and now you have given me a concrete sign that he is with me every day. You confirmed the pins he gave me, and the birthday card he wrote to me before his death.

I still go through ups and downs each day, but I carry that new comfort inside me. I have felt him clearly in our house so many times, and thanks to you, I know he is really there, and that it's not just my imagination.

Hopefully someday I will share time with someone new and special. But I also look forward to the day when I will see Maurice in Heaven.

Sincerely,

Lynn

But this love story doesn't end here. Here is what Lynn shared with me about her next amazing encounter with her soul mate.

On July 16, 2010, Lynn and Maurice's daughter Brittany married her beloved, Chad, in a garden ceremony. It was a hot, windless day, and the overcast sky threatened rain.

Lynn (wearing the fitted black dress, just as Maurice had suggested) waited with her daughter for their cue to walk into the garden. Many emotions reeled through her mind: joy, sorrow, and anticipation, all mixed together in a nervous jumble.

Brittany grabbed her mother's hand and whispered, "I wish Dad were here. I miss him so much!"

"He is here, honey," Lynn said assuredly. "He has always been here with us. We just can't see him."

As those words passed her lips, the clouds overhead parted, and sunlight poured down over the garden. A warm breeze ruffled their hair. Mother and daughter looked at each other in amazement.

The entrance music began to play. Lynn walked her trembling daughter out onto the garden path. As they drew closer to the trellis, she noticed that a butterfly had alighted on the unity table. Its multicolored wings fluttered gently.

"Brittany, look!" Lynn pointed. "Your father always did love to have the best seat in the house."

The butterfly remained perched on the table throughout the entire ceremony. Lynn and her younger daughter, Kristen, feeling Maurice's presence, began to cry. The guests, too, noticed this remarkable phenomenon, and the photographer snapped picture after picture.

When the pastor at last announced, "You may kiss the bride," the butterfly launched itself into the air, spiraling joyfully all around the gazebo. It was an awe-inspiring moment, a perfect testament to Maurice's love for his child and his blessing upon her marriage.

Later, during the reception, a cousin approached Lynn and said, "As you were leaving the garden, the butterfly came and perched on your chair. I snapped a photo of it sitting on the program, right on top of where it says, 'In Celebration of Brittany and Chad.' I just thought you'd want to know."

Truly, that day was a celebration of enduring love that no one in Lynn's family will ever forget.

*   *   *

We all have many angels. David, Irene, and Maurice have become angels for those who love them. Their presence reminds us that although our loved ones cannot always be with us in the flesh, they are fully present in spirit. We need only reach out to them, and be open to the miracles of love they show us every day!

CHANNEL 2

Fathers Follow You

The intimate significance of the father-child relationship does not change after one party is gone. From Heaven, fathers still act as our teachers, holding our hands in a spiritual sense just like they held our hands when we crossed the street as children. Those hands may even be extended again when it is our time to cross over to the other side.

Many times, fathers show up to help us fix what is broken in our lives. These things may be mundane: leaky faucets, broken windows, or sticky locks. At other times, fathers appear to address deeper issues like family dysfunction, guilt, or their absence while still physically in the world.

We are born with the need for unconditional love. In order to move forward, we have to prioritize the healing of our hearts over repairing the roof. We want answers, respect, forgiveness, and absolution. The spirits of fathers often appear to offer these things, whether we think we are ready for them or not!

A Father's Forgiveness

My longest private reading, which clocked in at more than three hours, was for a family of five who wanted to explore just this type of spiritual engagement. Ula, the mother, brought her four middle-aged children along for the reading so they could witness and validate the spiritual encounters she'd been having on her own. But when they sat down, the person who arrived wasn't a grandmother or family elder, but Ed, Ula's ex-husband, who had abandoned the family when his children were all under ten years old.

The moment Ed announced himself, the atmosphere in the room changed from one of openness to one of outright hostility.

It's not unusual for people to be nervous during channeling sessions, especially if they're first-timers. Sometimes it takes a while to diffuse any fears about death, or soften past the walls that grief can build. However, this was the first experience I'd had with this kind of spiritual Family Feud. I had never imagined a situation in which the spirit who entered my awareness wouldn't be welcomed.

"Is it okay for me to proceed?" I asked. "He is coming through very strongly."

The room was divided. Two of the siblings said yes, while the other two said "No way!" Ula was the deciding vote.

"Let him say what he has to say," she told me.

There was still clearly some major resistance happening here, but I'd gotten the go-ahead, so ahead I went.

Patiently, Ed began to call out to his family one by one. His daughter, Alice, he referred to as "Al-Al," his nickname for her when she was little. I could tell that he was grateful and happy to be able to deliver his message to his whole family at once, in a way that they couldn't misunderstand or ignore. This was an unprecedented reunion. It was beyond therapy; their emotional bodies were exposed.

He began with a sincere request for forgiveness. For forty-nine years, he'd been an absent father. Although he'd been deceased for thirty-four of those years, the hurt was obviously still fresh for his family. "I have been fossilized for three decades," he said through me. "I have been waiting for a chance to ask your forgiveness."

The general energetic tone from the family at this point was, "Yeah, right!" But Ed wasn't deterred. He showed himself to me with light skin and a potbelly, and personified his Irish heritage through a Claddagh ring. He mentioned numerous other family members and dogs that were with him on the other side of the veil. "I love shepherding animals and children," he said through me. He also mentioned Ula's cooking. "Thank you for providing meals for our family."

That comment made everyone laugh. "My cooking was never very creative," Ula explained, "But Ed always thanked me after every meal."

"He is still thanking you," I told her.

I received information from Ed that he left Ula and their four children for another woman and her family. As Ula confirmed this, her children's bitterness returned full force. Ed tried to soften it by sharing the names of animals that had crossed over in the last few decades. He also told Ula that he would be with her at her doctor's appointment on the Wednesday following the reading. "Could you please put some yellow flowers in the vase in the kitchen for me?" he asked. "Flowers like the ones at my funeral?"

Ula nodded. I could feel her resistance softening. "I know he's asking for my forgiveness," she told her children. "In his own simple way, he's asking."

Ed spoke next to the whole family. "I left because my departure made room for a new father figure to step into your lives. He was a healthy role model, and a better husband and father than I could have been. I know you felt abandoned and neglected, but things had to be that way."

"My second husband was a wonderful father figure," Ula agreed. "Maybe it really was for the best."

Spirits don't talk about their own feelings often, but they do talk about yours. They'll nudge you to free yourself from memories that you're holding in a negative way. This is the art and science of forgiveness, and the lesson that Ed was sharing through his communication. He offered several more confirmations, and accessed a few memories that weren't so painful for his family.

"Would it be okay if I visit again?" he asked, when the session was at last complete.

This time, the answer was a unanimous "Yes!"

Expect the Unexpected

I find myself falling in love with the spirits I meet on a daily basis. They don't have the human burdens and emotional peccadillos that the rest of us have. And because they have no reason to lie, hide, or elude, I can be certain that the messages they offer are aligned with the highest truth.

For most who come to my channeling sessions, just hearing that their fathers are following them in their daily lives is enough to make them gasp. But when I agreed to do a reading for Chris, an old friend and frequent flier at the Yoga Center, I knew that what came through would be more than just a mere acknowledgement of spiritual presence.

Chris carries a golden matriarchal aura around her even in broad daylight. I have come to recognize this golden light as a symbol of Christ consciousness. That term has multiple interpretations, but to me it simply shows a being who is devout in practice, and highly evolved in his or her own spirituality. Chris is certainly devout in her service to family, animals, and her community. When I told her that speaking to the deceased had become my purpose and passion, she laughed joyfully, and offered her congratulations. She seemed to have no discomfort whatsoever about the channeling process, or the fact that she has her own spiritual entourage. In fact, she couldn't wait to hear what her guides and ancestors had to say about her life and the direction in which she was taking it.

Nearly every channeling session ends up testing the edges of the client's mind, spirit, and emotions. These sessions encourage the resolution of tangled karma, the broadening of limiting beliefs, and the release of anything that is no longer serving.

I communicated this to Chris as we started our meditation. "I have a feeling that this reading is going to be adventurous for you," I warned her.

"I'm ready," she said firmly.

"Great! Because your father, Henry, is here. He's been waiting to speak to you."

Chris was caught completely off-guard. I could see internal grief and radical acceptance colliding in her emotional field. "Why him?" she whispered.

Estranged relationships in life create actual energetic distance between the two parties, especially when we try to put those certain souls out of our minds and hearts. Obviously, Chris had not been expecting this particular visitor. Just as obviously, this was a meeting that needed to happen.

"He's showing me his hand," I told her. "It's covered with psoriasis. He also says that you held his hands during the last moments of his life, and that this was a very powerful spiritual experience for you—a karmic experience."

Despite her distress, the relationship between Chris and her father was showing up to me in a rainbow of colors, as sometimes happens when family bonds are particularly strong.

"It was powerful," she said at last. "My dad was an alcoholic, and not always a good father. I was angry with him for a long time. But as he was dying, I realized that holding on to resentment was my choice, and I didn't have to do it anymore. I just... gave it up."

I was awed by her wisdom, and could feel Henry's pride in her. There's a false power in withholding our forgiveness, but in the end, hanging on to anger and resentment only creates a roadblock to our own heart's path. If the feelings are strong enough, they can even cause trauma in the physical body: issues in the tissues, madness in the muscles, and heaviness in the heart.

"Freeing yourself of your anger also freed me," Henry told his daughter. "I'm happy to see that you desire communication."

"Well, I don't know if I'd go that far..." Chris said, half-jokingly.

"I want to explain something," Henry continued through me. "While I was alive, it was very difficult for me to understand love. My mother died when I was little, and I lost my willpower growing up without her. There was no hand-holding. It was very easy for me to turn to 'liquid love.' She is with me now, though, and she's holding my hand—just like you held mine while I was transitioning."

Chris nodded. "I understand." A flood of tears ensued.

"This is a lesson to add reconciliation to your bucket list," I said as she wept. "What we resist persists. We need to offer forgiveness, for our own sakes."

When Chris was ready, Henry's transmission picked up once more. "I want to tell you that I'm proud of you for moving to Florida. It's making your husband really happy and sunny! You are a spiritual philanthropist in whatever community you live. You're doing your homework. The next step is for you to study healing touch or Reiki."

"I just got certified for Reiki level I," she confirmed.

"Don't forget the value of loving exchanges and forgiveness while you're on Earth. I'm still learning lessons about life here in the afterlife! And cherish your large family."

Chris has seven children and eighteen healthy grandchildren. She has great relationships with them all. "It's nice to know that he can see them," she said.

Henry stepped aside to let Chris's mother, Bernice, come through. "I'm in a different location than your father," Bernice said through me. "I'm receiving further education. I also want to say that I honor and admire the full capacity of the mother you've become."

"Oh my God, Those were the exact words she said to me right before she passed!" There was a look of wonder on Chris's face.

"It's time for you to share those words with your sister as well. She needs to hear them."

"I will," Chris promised.

"What is the significance of August eighteenth?" I asked Chris. "She's giving me that date as a confirmation."

"That's her birthday!"

Chris started her reading with her hand over her mouth in shock, overwhelmed by who was showing up, and how—and she ended the reading in the same way. "I never could have prepared myself for this messaging," she told me afterward.

"Spirit messaging is never going to give you more than you can integrate in the moment," I told her. "You were prepared for a powerful shift, and you got one!"

She wiped her eyes and laughed. "I sure did. I'm recycling my issues into the recycled tissues!"

Neighborhoods are a-Changin'

Our Teacher Training students at the Yoga Center end their year of study with a retreat at the Jersey Shore. I remember the group from 2012 in particular, because during the mediumship session on our first night two father figures came through quite clearly—although with very different energies.

Jodi had lost her father in an accident a few short weeks before our retreat, and was still coping with the wave of shock and loss which inevitably follows such a sudden transition. Throughout the whole meditation and the initial part of the session, I could feel her holding her breath, trying to "keep it together." But when her father entered the room, she and I exhaled simultaneously.

He offered his love to her, and let her know that he was safe and happy on the other side. He also remarked on the family piano, and how she needed help with moving it. "Don't just give it away," he said through me. "Keep it in the family. It's an heirloom."

Jodi explained to us her father's sentimentality, and how he was passionate about preserving memories. She was shocked that he had seen the piano being moved only a few days before. "He doesn't need to worry. I would never get rid of it."

"I will continue to watch over you," her father told her. "I will offer continuous guidance, if you are open to it."

"I am," Jodi said through her tears.

I looked around the room. Everyone had circled up in support of Jodi, and the tissue box was being passed around like a talisman. I had the impression that we—the sitters and I—were students in a classroom. The spirits who came to share their messages were our teachers.

I was then instructed to say to the group at the top of my lungs, "We're not in Mr. Roger's perfect Neighborhood anymore!"

At first, I wasn't really sure why this had come through. In case you haven't seen it, Mr. Roger's Neighborhood was a popular educational show in the 60s and 70s on PBS. It gave a lot of kids (including me) hope that there could be a kind, loving, dependable father figure out there. I remember clearly the way he would talk to me through the camera, asking questions, telling me I was special. I wasn't always noticed by my own father, but I was seen daily by Fred Rogers.

Looking around the room, I focused on Donna—and the spirit who was standing right behind her. "Someone is here for you, Donna," I said. "Are you ready to receive his message?"

The spirit stepped forward and introduced himself. His name was Fred—just like Mr. Rogers. I knew now where the reference had come from.

I could see Donna's shock, and suddenly recalled the conversation she and I had when she started her yoga teacher training. She'd shared that she was seeking a more consistent sense of inner peace now that many family obligations—including caring for her father during his last days—had been met. "If not now, when?" she'd asked.

Apparently, with Fred's appearance in our midst, the time for peace-making had come.

"I don't understand why he's showing up now," Donna said. "I finalized things, and buried any resentment, so why is he here, two years later?"

"Because it is perfect timing. He wants to ask your forgiveness now," I told her. "He couldn't ask before."

Fred showed me his lungs, a skeletal heart, and his dementia. "My heart wasn't full," he said through me.

It was like a bubble burst inside Donna. She started to sob.

"I have visited you before this," Fred told his daughter through me. "I appreciate your efforts to create balance with yourself and your family. Your care can't compare."

He acknowledged the cross hanging near the front door of the house Donna grew up in, and how he loved having visitors to the house. "He has strong social and religious values," I said.

"Yes. It seemed crazy to me that someone so religious could step over the line, get sloppy drunk, and act so terribly. It was totally dysfunctional."

As the session went on, it became clear that Donna still held tremendous judgment toward her father for things he had done in life which hurt her and her siblings. She still thought about the man he could have been, had he only been aware enough to try. There was a lot of hurt there to process, and it couldn't be done in the space of an hour-long channeling session.

I asked Donna if she would check in with me again as her healing progressed, and share any further messages she received from Fred in the coming weeks. "Instant messaging is developing!" I said.

As promised, Donna wrote out her version of events in the days after our session. She also explained more about her relationship with her father, and why his appearance at our session affected her so deeply.

> *The retreat at the Jersey Shore was wonderful. Our group is really like a family now, although it took a while for everyone to gel. In fact, when we made the plans to go on the retreat, I was lukewarm about the whole thing. But by the time the weekend arrived, I could hardly wait.*
>
> *After coffee on Saturday morning, we gathered in the family room, which overlooks the ocean. We all began to meditate, and Alaine began to write in her notebook. I knew she would be communicating with people who had passed away. I thought briefly about Jim, my first partner, and my dad, but I wasn't particularly interested in having anyone come through to communicate with me.*

When the meditation was finished, I listened with interest as Alaine spoke to others in the group. I was especially wrapped up in the messages for Jodi, whose dad had passed very recently. She seemed really happy to hear from him.

Then, I got a real shock.

Alaine said that someone had come for me. I assumed it was Jim, my "work husband" from years ago. But it was my dad. I felt like a shock went through my body, a visceral vibration that rocked me all the way to my core. I began to explain this feeling to my friends, but started to cry.

My dad was a tough cookie. I would absolutely say that he did not live up to my expectations about how a "good" dad should be. Intellectually, I understood his limitation. He'd had a hard life growing up, and provided for his family as best he could. He was a hard worker, a loyal friend, and generous to a fault. However, in the husband/father department, I always felt he came up short.

In the end, I was the one who nursed him through his many illnesses. His care, and the care of my mother, became my responsibility (my brother, for various reasons, was unable to help).

I did what I had to do, and accepted responsibility. I really did love my father, so I tucked the resentment away until his passing—but since then, on the rare occasions when I think of him, I have always been quick to see the bad, and push the good away.

And that's the way it's been for the last three years, until Saturday, when it all came rushing back.

As Alaine said, "We're not in Mr. Roger's perfect Neighborhood anymore."

My dad's name was Fred, and this was even more confirmation that he was in the room. It wasn't just a feeling for me; it was more of a "knowing." My body was still reacting to the internal shift of all that buried resentment. There were references to our front door, and religious symbols from our house. My dad always loved having company, even when they weren't invited! The message I took from this was that I needed to allow his presence inside, even though I hadn't invited him. I guess he's still teaching me lessons.

He also mentioned that "Your care can't compare." I took that as a reference to the care I've been giving my mom since his passing. I think he worried a lot about that at the end and is happy to see that she is well taken care of. It could also refer to the care I gave him, despite my harsh feelings, when he was ill.

Alaine explained several more things, but the one which stuck most was this: Fred may not have had the emotional tools to be his best self in life, but I do! Shifting this energy can help my dad be divinely celebrated. It isn't energy-efficient to store away bad feelings. I understand now that I have the power to rewrite my story—even to change the ending. I can open myself to the possibility that my relationship with my dad can still change and grow, even though he's no longer here physically.

The reading happened on Saturday. After I got home from our retreat, I remembered that my father's birthday had been on Friday—the day before he showed up in our session. It was another jolt! I felt ashamed that I hadn't even thought about him on his birthday. Maybe he knew, or felt, that. There are no coincidences.

It also made perfect sense that he would come to me near the beach. Any place near the ocean was his favorite place in the world. I have many happy memories of our family's summer vacations which I had forgotten until now. My father always played with my brother and me, carrying us into the water, jumping the waves, and playing wheel games on the boardwalk (during which he won me dozens of stuffed animals)! These are happy, loving memories that I'd chosen to bury beneath hurt and anger.

Now, all that anger seems a waste of bodily space. I am so grateful to have the opportunity to reexamine it all. It would seem that my story is finally finished, here, with this healing and resolution. But of course, it's not.

On Sunday night, I got the most intense and painful urinary tract infection of my entire life. I almost had to go to the emergency room. As my bodily drama played out through the rest of the week, I realized that I wasn't getting any better. The medication I'd gotten was making me sick, and I was forced to cancel all of my plans. I was so put out!

Then, I realized that the jolt I'd felt when Alaine channeled my father had seemed to come straight up through the core of my body. I felt that it had settled in my second chakra, the vortex of creation, creativity, and emotion. All the old hurt, anger, and resentment I'd released around my father were causing this infection! As this energy tried to make its way out of my body, it was literally making me sick, and forcing me to stay home and reflect.

I e-mailed Alaine, who told me that "This urinary tract infection is going to release you from being 'pissed off' forever!"

I pulled out all of my recent journals. Of course, the first one I opened was from the time of my dad's illness and death. As I read, I was able to see how the feelings I'd been holding on to had come from inside me, not from my dad. And if they were mine, I could choose to release them.

But the story still doesn't end there...

After a few more days, I felt well enough to have lunch with a couple of girlfriends. One of them, Lori, has had several sessions with Alaine, during which her father repeatedly showed up in his white doctor's lab coat. The difference between her experiences and my own was that she had been looking to speak with her father, and I had not. In any event, I told her my story, and we discussed the commonality of spirits, and how fathers seem to want to continue to parent, even from the other side.

That night, Lori sent me an e-mail. She'd heard a song earlier in the day by Paul Simon called "Father and Daughter." It's a song she loves, but doesn't hear very often. After we left the restaurant, she heard the song again! She knew that this was a message for me, and sent me a link to the song on YouTube. The moment I pressed "play," I started to cry. The lyrics were incredible! I was particularly struck by these words:

As long as one and one is two

There could never be a father who loved his daughter

More than I love you

I can't describe the love that filled my body. It was like my dad, who'd been unable to protect me while here on Earth, was finally able to make me feel loved and safe.

It was such a good feeling—one I'd been waiting for my whole life.

I know now that I can turn to my dad whenever I need him. I never did that while he was alive, because I knew he was not that person for me. But now it's clear: He is me, and I am him. Not only is my dad there for me, I am there for myself.

I'm not trying to wrap all this up in a neat little package with a pretty bow. I'm too much of a skeptic for that— and after all, we're not in Mister Roger's Neighborhood anymore! But I played that Paul Simon song over and over again, until I felt all the layers of defense loosen around my heart. During the last refrain, my dog Zoey was getting agitated, almost like she wanted to show me something. I followed her to the back door and across the patio, still hearing the song playing in the background. I wanted a sign.

Even as I looked up overhead, I knew what I would see: one beautiful shining star, directly over my head. It was amazing.

So that's the end of this story—or rather, the beginning. I couldn't make this stuff up if I tried. I'm not sure if I will connect with my dad again, but I feel that he is with me, watching over me, and for now that is enough.

Donna

CHANNEL 3

Bringing It Back to the Center

Fifteen years after we first opened our doors, and four years and 4,000-plus readings since I started offering channeling sessions, the Yoga Center of Medford has evolved into a Mecca for spiritual seekers. People come from all over New Jersey and beyond to experience a reconnection with their departed loved ones. It just goes to show that we are all looking for guidance and reassurance from the spirit world.

This seeking isn't always conscious; often, people come for a yoga class and leave with a channeled message from their dearly departed. Other times, they come despite their "better judgment"—like the woman whose ultra-religious father would never have set foot in a place like the Yoga Center. (When her father came through in our session, he was holding a Bible, so his daughter would recognize him, but he didn't object to being channeled in the least!) It's all about what each seeker is ready and willing to receive.

When we embrace the power of meditation and spiritual connection, we discover that we too can talk to our loved ones and receive the support and confirmation we need to create greater harmony in our lives. This one-on-one connection can happen organically, bit by bit, unfolding like an origami lotus. Or, it can happen spontaneously, all at once, like a supernova exploding in our consciousness.

Just like the planets in our solar system are always in motion, so are the planes of our consciousness. Almost every day, we wake up asking the same questions: Who am I? How am I? What is my greater purpose? Our past experiences and present knowledge intertwine to create the day's unique answer. Changing the way we perceive and experience life requires us to search for new and better responses to these questions. We can receive messages from the spiritual dimension which assist us in that search—but only when we're ready to hear them.

As the meditation sessions at the Center have continued to grow and evolve, I've learned that in order to get the most out of any spirit communication, both the sitter and I have to know what we know, and be hungry for what we *don't* know. Every message that comes through me is a designated piece of guidance for the recipient, regardless of its source. Sometimes, people want to "direct-dial" a particular loved one. That approach doesn't always work. There is no guarantee that the requested spirit will pick up the phone, so to speak—but what does come through will always be for the greatest good of the receiver, and anyone else who happens to be present.

Some of the most powerful messages I've received have been for, and from, people with a deep connection to the Yoga Center: our teachers and devoted students. Maybe it's because their energy is so deeply rooted in the space; maybe there's some other reason I can't yet fathom. The messages themselves have become part of the fabric of the Center as well—the folklore of our community, if you will.

The following are just a few of the stories that bring us "Back to the Center..."

The Man, the Message... The Leisure Suit?

One of the first lessons I received for myself as a practicing medium was, "Come out of the closet! Trust the spirit messenger, regardless of whose house you're in or where the delivery happens."

The first channeling session I led at the Yoga Center wasn't intended to be a session at all; rather, it was an informal early morning meditation. As we were putting our cushions away, I pulled one of the women aside.

"Gerri? Who would be standing behind you wearing a powder-blue leisure suit and waving a white handkerchief?"

"Oh, my God!" Gerri gasped. "That's my father! That blue suit was his trademark. And the last thing I put in his coffin was a white handkerchief!"

Spirits often use their appearance to give confirmation of their identity. They may come through as an exact replica of a photograph you look at regularly. They may share details from their funeral, or even use visual images to emphasize their strongest personality trait.

In this case, it was a little of everything. "Seems like your dad is really trying to get your attention," I observed.

Laughing and crying at the same time, Gerri nodded. "I was thinking of him during the last part of the meditation. I can't believe he showed up. And in that suit!"

I felt a beautiful calm settle over the room. This confirmation of her father's nearness had shifted Gerri's whole being. I felt "truth bumps" rising on my arms. (Truth bumps are like goose bumps, but they happen when there's a universal confirmation!) There was no detailed message: Dad was just dropping by to say hello, and let his daughter know he was with her.

Not every channeled message that comes through makes sense to me. Nor does it have to! Sometimes, the symbols, images, or words I receive seem random—but to the spirit's loved ones, they're powerful and meaningful. Gerri's dad showing up in a blue leisure suit seemed like a passing detail to me at first, but it was all the confirmation Gerri needed to receive her father's message of love.

Later, she told me that the powder-blue suit had been a constant in her father's life. "He wore it to my sister's first communion. He wanted to wear it to her wedding, too, but my mother put her foot down. After he passed away, we all went to the funeral home. Someone asked, 'What is he going to wear?' There was no question: we all said, 'The suit!'"

Gerri was also surprised that her dad would come to visit her at the Yoga Center, and not in his beloved church. A staunch Irish Catholic, he wanted nothing to do with any "unorthodox" spiritual practices while here on Earth—and yet there he was, waving his white handkerchief, beaming a jolly smile at his daughter as she chanted "Om" on her meditation cushion!

O Captain My Father

As I mentioned previously, spirits call out to you when you're ready to hear them. It's up to the medium to have specific office hours!

Al made his way into a yoga class that was not scheduled to have any otherworldly visitors. However, as I was opening myself more and more through monthly channeling sessions at the Center, a greater numbers of spirits were showing up on a daily basis. You know the saying: "When the student is ready, the teacher appears." I am always the student, it seems—even when I'm teaching!

If the Center is a beacon for spirits, it is also a refuge for those suffering loss. Stacey, a one-time student, lost her father in September of 2009. Struggling with her loss and the resulting depression, she hadn't been to a yoga class in three months. Nobody knew why she had been absent until December twenty-third, when the Center drew her back. She shared her story with us after that class, and returned several more times to participate in more formal channeling sessions.

Stacey later wrote about her experience.

Dear Alaine;

The first few months without my dad had me on an emotional roller coaster. I was filled with confusion and loss. We'd called him "Captain My Father." He really was the captain of our family's ship, and we would have done anything for him.

By the time Christmas rolled around, I wasn't feeling any better, but I felt an extreme pull to come to the Yoga Center for a class. I was expecting the regular teacher, but Alaine happened to be substituting. I warned her about my emotional state beforehand, just in case I broke down in tears during the practice.

At the end of the class, Alaine decided to try a "different" meditation. What came through was a healing, peaceful message.

"Stacey," she asked. "Who's Al?"

Immediately, I started to cry. "My dad. He's my dad."

"He's with his friends. They're speaking for him, since he's not ready. He wants you to know that he's okay."

It made total sense that my dad would step back and let others speak. Despite his social nature, he was a man of few words, especially when it came to deeply emotional issues.

I left the Center that night with an incredible feeling of peace that stayed with me throughout the holidays. Thank you, Alaine, for such an incredible Christmas gift!

During other group sessions, more strong messages came through. During one, you said that he liked his belly jiggling. I related that to my memory of the night he died. The paramedics administered CPR, and every time they pumped his heart, his belly jiggled. I believe that he sent that message to let me know that he's happy where he is, and that I don't have to think of his dying as a "bad" memory. He's really okay now.

I also had a dream about him reaching his hand through my childhood bedroom door. He delivered a message through you that it was his hand I saw. It kind of blew my mind that he knows what I'm dreaming. It's wild!

Every message I've received from my dad has been very healing. I know that my relationship with him continues even though I can't physically be near him or hug him. There are times when I get confused or start to lose direction, but when I get these messages from my dad, I know that he is still there to give me guidance and encouragement.

I collect books, but I'm not always very good about reading them. He's told me that I should follow through with my goal of reading more. I also think he's sending me messages through some of the books. The Last Song *is a great example. It's about a girl whose father dies. While playing the piano at his funeral, she looks up at the stained glass window overhead, and sees a sunbeam shining through. She knows it is her dad, smiling down at her from Heaven. I think my dad wanted me to read this book so I would know that he, too, is always smiling down on me.*

Stacey

F-R-E-D

F-R-E-D: he spelled out his name for me. Yes, he assured me, he spelled it correctly! But he first let his presence be known by the color of his son's bedroom walls.

He made me ask, "Whose bedroom walls are bright yellow?" Like, who's the fool who would paint his walls such a silly color? He pressed me to add, "And I see your romantic interludes there, by the way."

Myles, a first-timer at the Center, recognized his father's sarcastic tone immediately. When I described F-R-E-D and his Archie Bunker mentality, his son's eyes welled up. "It's totally like my father to talk about sex and decorating!"

Myles's fiancée Natalie, seated beside him, blushed. "I can't believe he can see us!"

Fred just kept talking, as if he was once again holding court at his Sunday dinner table. "No such thing as waiting for marriage anymore, huh?" he quipped.

But beyond the teasing, I could feel the outpouring of love that Fred felt for his children—for Myles, the spitting image of his father, and his daughter Laurie, the apple of his eye.

"I had biases about men's and women's roles," Fred shared through me. "You'll know what I mean when you have your own daughter. And you don't have to worry about getting the diseases I had. You don't have my threatening habits."

I got the sense that Fred liked being in the male body. He was fearless with his indulgences: drinking, eating, smoking, driving fast.

"Men are supposed to do battle, even with themselves," he explained to me. I didn't argue.

"Take care of your mother," he told Myles. "Help her with her hip and knee issues, but let her walk her own path. And make sure she gets to the casinos every once in a while!" Myles smiled tearfully at that: one of his parents' favorite pastimes had been to travel to Atlantic City and gamble pocket change.

"Now," Fred said through me. "Where is my picture? I'm not getting any recognition!"

Myles and Natalie looked at each other and burst out laughing. "It's in the spare bedroom," Myles told me. "I had a feeling he wouldn't like it there. But he'll always have a shrine in me."

"It's not artificial?" Fred asked me to say.

"No, it's not." Mike opened his shirt to reveal a beautiful tattoo across his chest. The design was obviously chosen in honor of his father.

Apparently satisfied, Fred mentioned the month of his own birthday, which is the same month that his grandsons (Myles's nephews) were born. "Just a little prodding to get your own family started." He also confirmed the date of Mike and Natalie's wedding in September.

"I expect a baby in April," he said.

"A baby conceived before the wedding?" I joked. "Does he expect Immaculate Conception?"

Myles laughed. "My brother was conceived before my parents' wedding. It's been a family 'secret' for years!"

The Boys in the Band

Spirits often come through in the way that they are personally viewed by the sitter. They show up in a way that their loved one can recognize, in the guise that will have the most impact for their emotional "rescue mission." Often, the same spirit will come through for a sitter multiple times over multiple readings, each time with a new outfit, physical appearance, or primary feeling. These manifestations are triggers designed to encourage recognition and trust in the spirit's message.

More rarely, a single spirit will appear at different times to multiple sitters. When this happens, the differences in how the spirit shows up are even more pronounced, because each person viewed the deceased so differently when he or she was alive. This was illustrated to me by the spirit of Seth, a seventeen-year-old boy who died in a terrible auto accident a few months before this particular group session.

Seth's mother arrived at our session scared and skeptical. I expected no less from a woman who'd so tragically lost a child. I don't believe that skepticism is a road block for spiritual contact; usually, the spirit just chooses another way to establish contact, one that doesn't allow for doubt.

It seemed like Seth's mom had decided on just a few "codes" which would prove to her that her son was in the room—and Seth didn't give them to me. In fact, he didn't speak to me at all. Rather, the elders around him spoke for him, offering light and rather vague confirmations and messages. I'd never seen this group effort before, especially for such a young and vibrant spirit. It was as though Seth was reluctant to stand out in the crowd.

Despite the near-total lack of information I was receiving, I was able to describe Seth quite well. At the end of the reading, his mother gave me a picture of him, taken only weeks before his death. "You can keep this if you want to."

"I'd be honored to keep it," I said.

For days, Seth was on my mind. I felt so connected to this young boy. I found myself sitting for long periods of time at my desk, staring at his picture, frustrated that I couldn't offer more to his grieving mom. What should I have done differently? What more could I have gleaned from my glimpses of him?

I knew patience would reveal an answer.

It dawned on me that I'd heard about Seth's passing, but hadn't connected it to the picture in front of me. The crash had happened in the community adjacent to ours, and Seth was the same age as my twins. In fact, a few of my children's schoolmates had been in a band with him. There were so many people grieving for this wonderful, vibrant child. My heart felt connected to the event of his death in a way that was hard to get over.

Patience is a virtue, they say—and time is a mental construct. I spent what felt like weeks ruminating over that picture. Finally, I had to put it away. When Seth was ready to show himself to me again, he would. I just had to trust the process.

Several months later, I booked a private reading for a mother and her two children. I don't know whom they were hoping to communicate with—but Seth came through before I could even get the session rolling. I recognized him immediately, even though I had no idea why he was there.

As it turned out, Mark, the older son, had been one of the kids in Seth's band. Unlike Seth's mother, Mark wasn't skeptical at all. He was excited to hear from his best friend.

Seth spoke. "I can come through for you, Mark, because we're of the same generation and our beliefs are different than those of our parents. I sit over your shoulder, right near your tattoo. And I want to give a shout out to Issac and Ryan, and that girlfriend you and I shared."

Mark smirked. "Don't say anything I wouldn't want my mom to know about."

"There's no pressure for old mistakes here, right?" I asked.

"No," Mark's mom agreed. "Whatever we say here can stay here."

I felt Seth's mischievous grin very strongly. "He seems like quite the little instigator," I said. "He had no fear. He must have been a great friend to have adventures with!"

"He was," Mark agreed.

Seth offered more confirmation. "The two of you ran for office in eighth grade," I said. "President and Vice President. You had pins and buttons and everything!"

Mark snorted. "It was our first and last attempt to save our class! No one voted for us, but it was a great time anyway."

"He also wants to remind you about the jacket you share."

"Yeah, he played football with me one year. We ended up winning the State Championship, and we've got the jackets to prove it."

As we talked, I could see Mark's despair at his best friend's passing begin to lift. Our conversation took on the tone of friendly banter so common to teenaged boys.

"I see your useless attempts to write lyrics about your losses," Seth said through me. "Don't worry, you'll write something passable soon."

"I can't believe you see that!"

"I see a lot. But this honor code we have is eternal, it will never go away. Think about how it has shaped your life. You'll never take anything for granted anymore. You've always believed in something larger than yourself. You've already captured the essence of unconditional love. So go write about that, man!"

This was the nature of their relationship. They never held anything back from one another. I felt privileged to be able to be a part of this boyhood bond of trust.

"Give my love to my mom," Seth asked through me. After offering the July date of her birthday as confirmation, he added, "Her grief is different than yours. I couldn't talk to her like this."

"Seth was always kind of a mama's boy, always protected by her," Mark told me. "All of us used to tease him about it."

At that point, it became crystal clear to me why Seth hadn't shown up fully for his mom: she hadn't wanted to share him with anyone, let alone a room full of strangers. The initial reading was protected, in a way, by that energy. She hadn't really wanted anything but confirmation that he was safe in Heaven; anything else would have felt like a breach of privacy. It was absolutely her right to put a hold on the communication during that first session: it was my own immaturity that had caused confusion.

Seth's mother has never come back for another reading. I don't mind. It's her privilege to connect with her son in her own unique way, without any outside interference. My two experiences with his spirit were lessons I'll never forget. Spirits always have their reasons, even when we don't understand them. All we can do is trust that their perfect messages will be revealed in the perfect time, in the perfect way, and using the appropriate media.

Obie!

Animals are just as powerful as humans in terms of their capacity for unconditional love, and their loyalty can last long beyond death.

Obie bounded into the room immediately after I opened our group channeling session. A twelve-pound ball of white fur, he ran straight to his owner, Julie, exactly as he would have in life. Despite the fact that many people in the room were new to channeling, almost everyone felt the joyful "puppy love" burst through the door.

Before I could even begin to share what I was seeing, Julie was already a mess of tears. Obie was running circles around her, practically flying: an exuberant lover reunited with his beloved. It's rare that human spirits have this kind of magnetism. Human relationships are complicated. So much is held in reserve. This definitely wasn't the case with Obie! It was as if he'd been waiting at the gates of Heaven for me to throw the bone toward his owner. Of course, he cut straight to the front of the line for channeling, claiming all of the attention, just as he would have in life.

"This is exactly what I needed to feel today," Julie said. "It's so funny to say this about a dog, but Obie and I had an amazing relationship." The pet owners in the room nodded understandingly at that. Julie's loss was as profound as any other.

Obie grinned a doggie grin, and I laughed out loud.

Julie's grandfather came through next, as though Obie had smoothed the way for him to enter the room. "Sailor blue for you," he asked me to say.

"My grandfather would always ask me if I was 'feelin' blue,'" Julie confirmed. "His last name was Saylor, and most of the family had "Saylor blue" eyes. I didn't get that gene."

"He wants to share his gratitude for the loving care you gave him in the hospital, and while he was passing. Obie is keeping him company now."

"Obie would do that," Julie said.

I remember that night as one of the most joyful sessions I've ever facilitated. The whole room was enveloped in animal spirit. Obie remained by Julie's side for the rest of the session, departing only when I formally switched off the spiritual channel. The last thing I saw was his little white tail, wagging furiously as he darted out the door and back to his heavenly doghouse.

I guess all dogs really do go to Heaven!

CHANNEL 4

It's Wisdom for "Shore"

The Jersey Shore seems to be a favorite gathering ground for spirits who want me to deliver messages for them. Judy's nephew David, whom we met in Channel 1, was just one of many loving beings who chose to reach out to me during beach vacations. Maybe it's the presence of the Atlantic Ocean, a powerful force in so many people's lives. Maybe it's my own openness when I'm removed from the day-to-day bustle of managing the Yoga Center and my family's schedule. Whatever the case may be, I've had a lot of unexpected house guests over the years.

One of these visitations occurred during a family reunion at the Jersey Shore. At the time, yoga was still viewed as cultish, a pursuit for hippies and heathens—or, worse, vegetarians. While my immediate family was aware that I could communicate with those beyond the veil,

I'd had to grow a thick skin against ridicule by my more conservative aunts, uncles, and cousins when it came to my "alternative" lifestyle choices. Let's just say that raw foods and spicy spiritual gatherings have never been the norm for my relatives!

Unbeknownst to me, I was about to "come out" over the course of this reunion weekend in a big way—by facilitating a spiritual reunion between my cousin, Jeffrey, and his recently deceased best friend, Rory.

Before we continue, let me share a little bit about my cousin. "Loud Long Island Jeff" is not a yogi by any stretch of the imagination (or body). In fact, one of his most infamous quips is, "I've never met a vice I didn't like!" His energy is highly charged—so much so that he once knocked out the power at our cousin's house the moment he knocked on the door. But he also has a heart of gold, and enough love for his family and friends to fill Long Island Sound. No family gathering could ever be dull with Jeffrey around.

Needless to say, I was quite surprised on this particular weekend when he slipped through the door of our house on the Jersey Shore without so much as a spark to announce him. It was late, and I was yawning but determined to wait up for his arrival. When I saw his face, I wondered if he was sick. Then, I saw a stranger standing behind him: a middle-aged man, handsome but sort of distorted, as if he'd been projected out of a funhouse mirror. No spirit had ever appeared this way to me before. Nor had I ever seen a spirit so clearly tailing someone. Where Jeffrey went, this stranger followed like a gray shadow.

Saying hello to an uninvited ghost in that crowd would have been more than socially inappropriate. Busting on each other might be a family pastime, but "ghost busting" is a game we've never played. Still, I couldn't ignore what was happening. The energy of this spirit was louder even than Jeffrey, and I knew I had to find a way to speak out despite the social circumstances.

I decided to sleep on it, so I said goodnight and went upstairs to bed. I tossed and turned all night. In my mind's eye, I kept seeing the handsome but haunted features of the spirit who'd followed Jeffrey through the front door.

In the morning, bleary and unsettled, I went downstairs for breakfast, where I got the lowdown from the aunts and uncles. Jeffrey's longtime friend, Rory, had recently committed suicide. It was a terrible story to hear.

I remembered Rory; I'd met him about five years previously. He'd been a forty-year-old MIT (millionaire-in-training) who seemed to have it all: good looks, personality, education, a beautiful wife, and three loving kids. His family business, which consisted of several car dealerships, was booming, and it provided a luxurious lifestyle.

From the conversational buzz happening in the kitchen, I gathered that, under the veneer of success and happiness Rory had presented, there was a lot of strife. The business that provided so much monetary wealth to his family was a source of serious stress and dysfunction. Rory was haunted by his elders' skewed views on wealth and power, but couldn't shed his golden handcuffs. Drugs, drinking, and destructive behaviors became his coping mechanisms. Anyone who didn't allow themselves to be pulled into this spiral simply got spun out of Rory's life—including Jeffrey, his best friend of twenty-two years.

Rory's existence of guilt, pain, and anger finally came to an end just days before our family reunion. Unable to cope with the reality of his life situation any longer, Rory drove his car to the local playground, parked, aimed a handgun under his chin, and pulled the trigger. His body was found hours later, slumped over the steering wheel.

Jeffrey was tortured. He hadn't been able to stop Rory's downward spiral before it claimed him permanently, and now he'd lost his best friend. They'd had an argument over Rory's drug use a couple of years before, and it had created an insurmountable wall between them.

The guilt Jeffrey carried over what had just happened dampened his usually bright light until it was barely a flicker.

It was now abundantly clear to me who Jeffrey's spiritual stalker was. I realized that Rory looked different to me because he'd died so violently. I challenged him to step forward and deliver his message, and was told to ask Jeffrey a few questions.

"I want to be sure we have his permission," Rory whispered to me.

I was still hesitant. I mean, Jeffrey was upset enough without me stepping in and adding more complications. But Rory wasn't going to leave without having his say. I decided that I would proceed, but tread carefully. If at any point I met resistance, I would shut down the communication. This was not a situation where I—or a spirit—could afford to be pushy.

Spirits, like human beings, work in mysterious ways. Sometimes, multiple spirits work in tandem to orchestrate serendipitous meetings and interactions. Rory, desperate to deliver a message to his friend, my cousin, must have called in some outside help, because in what seemed like no time at all I found myself walking on the beach alone with Jeffrey and my dogs. We sat on the dunes, looking out over the gray-blue waves.

Once we were settled, I carefully broached the subject of channeling. "This might come as a bit of a shock," I said, "But I have a couple of questions I'm supposed to ask you. Your answers will let me know if I have permission to speak further about a spirit who's following you. We don't have to talk about this if you don't want to," I hurried to add.

"Questions?" Jeffrey asked. "What kind of questions?"

"I think you'll know when I ask them. They don't have to make sense to me, only to you. After we're done, you can tell me if you want to proceed. Okay?"

"You got it."

"The first question is about jackets, and jackets."

Jeffrey was silent.

"The second is, have you found any change on the floor lately? And the third—" I took a deep breath. "How was such a violent act completed in such a clean way?"

"You're talking about Rory," Jeffrey confirmed. "He was wearing a white shirt. The shot was so clean that there was hardly any blood. And the jackets... He was buried in two jackets. One was his silver sailing jacket. He loved that jacket. The other was the black jacket he was wearing when he shot himself. It didn't get released from the police department until the day of the wake. They couldn't get the silver jacket off, so they just put the black one on over it."

My gentle giant of a cousin wiped tears from his eyes. I could tell he was a little overwhelmed.

I patted his arm. "I'm going to write down more messages from Rory when we get back to the house. His spirit is very local, but he felt he needed permission from you to trespass. He's got a lot to say, and it will come through more clearly if I write it down. Can we take some time later to go deeper?"

I felt like I was sealing some sort of bargain between the souls of these two friends. I prayed for this messaging to come through in the most efficient, effective, and loving manner. I was used to working in raw emotional environments, but this was new territory for me. I had to trust in my own integrity to see this through.

Back at the beach house, I sat down at the table in my room with a pen and notebook. I filled page after page with Rory's channeled messages. Some of it made perfect sense to me, and some of it made no sense at all. Some of it came in the form of a letter; other parts were more a stream of feelings and impressions. I wrote it all out anyway, trusting that this collection of words would convey all of Rory's intended meaning to Jeffrey.

Several hours later, Jeffrey and I returned to the dunes. I opened my notebook, and when my cousin indicated he was ready I started to read Rory's heartfelt words out loud.

"Sorry, very low to the ground. My heart was heavy for all, more than just myself. My lesson is to love and accept myself as I was not what I wanted to be in this life. I am full of regret, but have lightness for you. I know I cannot say "I'm sorry" and ease the damage I did to our friendship while I was living. I never could have known the light like I do now.

"My heaviness is now being drawn down by my family. Their heavy hearts match how mine used to feel daily."

As I read Rory's words about his heavy heart aloud to Jeffrey, I felt that heaviness intensely through my whole body.

"Yes," I continued, *"You did see me through your doorway around your night table. I visited with you, but now it's part of my transition to move on. You will be moving on also, but that doesn't mean that we can't still feel each other. Please remember me as I was before I lost my mind to drug use. You tried to help, but it was no use, I was unsalvageable. I was in my own living hell, and it was only the love you and my family had for me that tempered the pain. Don't take on any guilt or responsibility for not being able to save me."*

"I did see him the other night, in my bedroom," Jeffrey told me. "It was like seeing a shadow of the guy he used to be. I wish he would have just talked to me, let that fight go!"

"He sees the anguish you're in," I said. "Maybe he couldn't face your feelings in life because he couldn't manage his own."

I continued to read. *"Please tell my wife Jenna that it's taking a while for my true transition, but I am here with my grandparents, 'R' and 'M.' who are pulling me into a better place. I ask that she embrace me—my better self, not the self I was at the end. I don't have regrets because I have been relieved of them; I hope that she can relieve herself of her regrets, too."*

"You've stayed friends with his wife, haven't you?" I asked. "I get the sense that he trusts you to tell her about this visit. Did you recognize the initials of his grandparents?"

"Rory was his grandfather's name, too. And his grandmother was Marla. He talked about them a lot."

"Please ask Jenna to sit at the end of our bed and see my statue/ image over the television. She should also read the book on the bottom of the stack first, since it's more relevant. I like the title better. Leave my love note as the bookmark. Tell her that I treasure the amazing love we had before my demise. I am learning self-love, and I will help her to do the same."

"Um, okay. I'll tell her." Jeffrey looked confused, but I knew that he would keep his word.

"I can't feel my children; I was numb for so long, and they didn't get the best of me. The remainder of my family is just a 'Shelly.' Please let them know when they are ready that I am giving much effort here toward cleansing my soul, and I will be looking for them when they are ready to see me again.

"Do you know what he meant by 'Shelly,'" I asked. "I feel like there's something in there he expects you to recognize."

"Michelle. Shelly is his twin sister. He used to call her his 'better half.'"

"I also feel that he saw himself as a shell of a man, toward the end. Empty." I shook my head, saddened. *"To you, my brother, Jeffrey: know that your heart is perfectly in the right place. You have been tested early in life. Confirmation is the name of your street, Hillcrest. Honesty and loyalty could have prevented what happened to me. That I 'see saw.'"*

I had a good idea of what this "testing" referred to. Jeffrey had lost his parents early in his life. I also saw the reference in the "see saw" to the playground where Rory's life ended—the same playground where his own kids once played freely.

There was more brotherly advice. I felt Rory's presence strongly with us, there on the beach. I read his words with the same brotherly tone he might have used with Jeffrey, back in the day when they used to shoot the breeze on bar stools.

"Go to the park more often, man. Begin your own self-preservation. You don't want to be where I am too soon. Other people need you now. There's not a sense of "missing" on this side, just an awareness of the value of relationship and the division death can bring. The mind isn't separate, here in Heaven. There are no comparisons of physicality, only differences of wisdom.

"It's good that you have another new dog."

Jeffrey laughed. "No way. I just got that dog yesterday. I haven't even told anybody about him yet!"

"Man's best friend," I quipped, and then continued, smiling. *"Thanks for being open to my being around. It will take more time and trust for me to be able to reach my family. Jenna needs more time to remove her anger around my selfish actions. It was a beautiful life that was created around me, but it wasn't really mine in the end. She will be taken care of, with lots of green around her. You are the man of the hour for her. Please look after all of my children, they will need emotional support. C-ya See ya Sea ya!"*

Tears and breath mingled with the lapping of the waves. I handed Jeffrey the letter. He read it several more times, as if hearing me speak the words hadn't made them real enough.

"I really feel him here, on the beach," my cousin said at last. "We used to spend summers on his family's boat, back when he was, you know, *himself.* We had so much fun."

"He's still here with you," I said. "If you're open, he'll keep showing up."

"I'd like that."

Jeffrey called Jenna to share Rory's letter with her. He hung up the phone with a lopsided grin on his face. His big hands were shaking, but his energy felt megatons lighter. "So, the statue you talked about, the one across from the bed on the TV, was actually a picture I took of the two of them on the deck of their boat. We were right in front of the Statue of Liberty. I asked her about the books on the nightstand, too, and you know what the bottom book was? *When Bad Things Happen to Good People*! That was the book Rory wanted her to read. Can you believe it? That is *so* crazy!"

Yup. Loud Long Island Jeff was back, full force. Just knowing that his friend was alright—that he still existed, even though his earthly body was shattered—was all he needed to jump start his emotional recovery process. Rory, in his own way, had been liberated by death. He was truly in a better place.

I leaned over to give Jeffrey a hug, and nearly got my ribs crushed as my cousin squeezed me in exhilarated relief.

Do we have the power to heal our emotional wounds while here on Earth? I think we do—and when we're ready, we can ask for help from the spirit realm. At some level of awareness, I know that Jeffrey and Rory's wife Jenna were asking for such help, and Rory came through loud and clear for them in this channeled letter. Still living the aftermath of his own destruction, Rory was ordained as a spirit guide. He is more at ease now, in the space of spirit wisdom and without the demands of an earthly body.

For my part, I was both shaken and deeply moved by this experience. There were so many "firsts" involved. Talking to Rory's spirit through my own doubts around family acceptance was a big step toward unity, and reinforced my trust around serving those I love. The deep affection and brotherhood that came through Rory's transmission has stayed with me ever since, a reminder that healing continues beyond the doors of death.

The Front Porch Diaries

One of the most memorable group readings I've conducted happened on the front porch of Alice's beach house on the Jersey Shore. Alice is a yoga teacher at the Center, and so it seemed natural to her to invite me to offer a channeling/meditation session to a group of her girlfriends during one of their weekend retreats.

Witnessing this group of friends together was a joy in and of itself. They had been friends since college and had supported one another through all of life's expected (and unexpected) events—engagements, weddings, breakups, divorces, births, and deaths. As a whole, they were extremely open to this channeling session, but no one could have guessed how their story lines would unfold on that sunny Shore afternoon.

We meditated together on the wide porch, with the sounds of birds, boats, waves, and windblown grass surrounding us. Immediately, a number of spirits showed up to be heard. It felt like this was a long-anticipated gathering—at least on the heavenly side!

"Jane," I said, addressing a woman sitting to my right, "It's clear that someone really wants to speak to you. She waited until the meditation was over to introduce herself, because she feels you need more quiet time in your life. She's a sweet, fun energy to receive. She's showing me her name as Nanna-An."

Jane beamed. "It's my mother! Her name was Ann!"

"She's anxious to communicate with you. There are a lot of trucks showing up behind her."

"Wow! My family is in the trucking and transport business!"

"She says that she's here with Poppy. He's very short. He also thanks you for holding his hands and heart in his last moments."

Jane's eyes teared up at that. "I can feel them here."

After that loving reunion, the two guides moved me toward Jane's denser energy. "Your emotional block is your resentment toward your ex-husband, Alan," I said. "William and Mary are here with you, too. They are caring for their grandson still, and for you."

"My ex's *grandparents* are looking out for me? Why?"

"Love isn't just for family. It's for in-laws and out-laws, too." The words came from William and Mary. I could feel their staunch, old-fashioned goodness enveloping the porch like a well-used quilt. "Relationships deteriorate on the earthly plane, but there are still lessons to be learned from those on the other side. We want you to know that Alan's education was the issue. This isn't about formal education: he needed to learn to love more in a marriage. He is learning that now. This isn't about looking at a broken marriage, but seeing a stepping stone into further soulful exploration."

Jane seemed in a stupor as she tried to process this information. When she didn't respond, I went on, still speaking for William and Mary. "We encourage you to follow your passions for cooking, gardening, and writing. Honor the achievements you have accomplished. Now, what is the thing on your bedside table that is very, very red?"

"It's a Bible from my family. It's in a red pencil case."

"This is a symbol of spiritual beliefs that were taught to you when you were young. That's why you put the book away in the case. Now you can determine your own beliefs. Sometimes, our circumstances change, and our beliefs need to change with them. You can write your own bible of life. Create your own personal faith by loving and caring for yourself first, and then others."

Jane's guides faded away, having delivered their compassionate message. After a moment, my gaze was drawn to Marilyn. "Why are there so many angels behind you?" I asked. "They feel very motherly. I'm also getting the letter 'L,' a name."

"My mother used to make angels when I was younger. It was kind of a hobby for her. Her name was Laura."

"She says that she smoked, and that she was taller in life than I'm seeing her now. She also says that you will know her by her flower essence, lilac."

Marilyn nodded. "She loved lilacs. She was always cutting them and putting them in vases around the house."

"She was very into the spices of life. She says I should mention a spicy chicken dish."

"My husband is Moroccan. She always referred to him as 'spicy.' I thought it was so cute. And he does make an amazing chicken tagine."

"She's mentioning the poems, and the turtle. She says she taught you to respect all life."

"Oh, my God! I can't believe she knows about the turtle! It only happened yesterday!"

The whole porch turned eagerly to look at Marilyn.

"Just this morning she was telling us how she always stops for animals in the road," Alice told me.

"Yes. I was trying to save a turtle yesterday. He just didn't want to get in my car!"

"Your mother wants me to also mention Hammonton, New Jersey. She's also showing me the number eleven—two ones, two artsy people, polar opposites. She says you need to fill the gap."

"My twin sister and me. That's who she's talking about. My sister is bipolar, and she still lives in Hammonton. We haven't been close since Mom died."

"Thank you for being willing to talk to angels," Laura said to her daughter through me. "You have a beautiful composure, growing love and laughter!"

Certainly Marilyn was laughing now. Her mother's lilac lightness surrounded the whole gathering as we took in the message of love.

It was Joellyn's turn next. "There's someone behind you who wants to be recognized by her eyes or eyeglasses," I said. "Do you know who that could be?"

"It's my mom, Phyllis." Joellyn confirmed. "She loved her glasses! She would even wear her favorite sunglasses in the house!"

"It's more than that," I said. "Deeper."

Joellyn nodded. "I looked right into her eyes before she died. We shared our last moment together that way."

"She's showing me a black dog. And asking me to say, 'Jack-in-the-Box.'"

"Jacques! He was our black poodle. I put a picture of him in her coffin with her."

"He's with her now, in the afterlife."

"I hoped that he would find her. They loved each other so much."

"She wants to extend her compliments on your unusually large wedding cake. I see a cake that keeps growing and growing."

Joellyn took a moment to ponder this. "Oh, I get it! My mom was always talking about the challenges of long-term marriages. She wasn't able to stay with anyone for very long. But I've been married for thirty-nine years."

"Some conversations between mothers and daughters never change," I smiled. "But she wholeheartedly approves of your husband."

"I know."

Phyllis stepped aside, and a different, younger energy came in. "Your son—did he have an 'R' in his name?"

"His name was Andrew."

"He says that his birthday was in May, and that he passed over from drug abuse. But you are being taught by his love for you from beyond. You are seeing pearls of wisdom from above."

I saw Joellyn fingering a pearl necklace. When she noticed me watching her, she nodded, understanding. "I wear this all the time. It was my mom's."

"Are you doing wisdom work?"

"I'm teaching grief counseling and supporting drug education in Andrew's memory."

"Andrew asks me to tell you that he was always the most free-spirited of your kids. He wasn't afraid of the dark, but now he's walking in the light, teaching you and learning from you."

Joellyn blinked back tears. "Thank you."

Dana's messages came through next. Although she'd voiced at the beginning of our session that she wanted to connect with her immediate family (especially her mother and father), it was her brother-in-law, Steve, who came through. He wanted Dana to deliver a message to his wife (Dana's sister), who wasn't present at the gathering.

"Steve is so happy you are here," I told Dana. "And that you're open and willing to receive his communication. He wants to thank you for honoring him during his passing from lung cancer. As confirmation, he reminds us that he's an Aries, born in April."

"Yes, that's Steve," Dana said.

"He's showing up in his bathing suit." I smiled at the vision. "He loved the shore, seafood, and boating."

"We used to have family gatherings up in Nantucket, Massachusetts. It was a total beach experience."

"He's showing me the initials 'J' and 'K.'"

"Those are his children's names. Jonah and Kelby," Dana confirmed. Tears formed in her eyes. "I'm so glad he's here. We had a special relationship, like we were really brother and sister."

"Steve says that he's at peace, and that he has the ability to watch over his family in a different way now. He says you can toss away the buckets of worry in your body. He's really doing fine."

I literally saw the release of tension from Dana's body as she cried.

Next, her parents showed up, right at the bottom of a heart. "They're together on Cloud Nine, and still very connected," I shared. "I'm also getting visions of battle scenes and men in uniforms."

"My mom was one of three sisters," Dana told us. "They all married soldiers and they were all married for over fifty years."

"This represents unbelievable commitment and a unique family bond. They're reminding you to treasure it. They're also showing me a piece of jewelry that was stolen. It doesn't matter that it was never recovered: it was a symbol of love, and that is still strong."

"Wow. I can't believe they showed you that! I made a bracelet for my sister years ago, and someone stole it."

The brother-in-law stepped back into my line of vision, and spoke through me. "I want to remind you about the family reunion on Nantucket this summer. You'll see your sister there, so you can tell her about this communication. I'll be there. You won't have to look for me: I'll find you. My symbol is a dragonfly."

"My sister still uses a dragonfly on her e-mail signature, even though Steve's been gone for twelve years."

"Maybe it's time for her to find a new love in her life, and stop looking back for the old one," I suggested.

As the reading came to a conclusion and everyone started chatting about their individual experiences, Dana struggled to pull herself together. "Do you really think I can share this with my sister?" she asked the group. "How can I tell her that Steve came to see me and not her? How will I know it's the right time?"

We all took a deep breath together—and watched as a huge dragonfly flew right past Dana's nose.

I smiled. "You'll figure it out."

AA: Ascended Archangels

There's a sweet yoga studio at the Jersey Shore where I offer sessions while I'm in town. During my first session there, I channeled several spirits who were surrounding a young man named Jay.

"There are five people wanting to get connected to you," I told him. "Their initials are Bs, Ws, and As. Some are duplicated. They're in a boat, and they're throwing you a life preserver. Do you know them?"

As this was his first experience with spirit communication, Jay was caught totally off-guard, and had no idea of the identity of these spirits who were vying for his attention.

"Don't try to make this fit with those who you are specifically trying to reach," I suggested. "These may be connections that you've forgotten about. There's one man in particular who says you would discuss movies with him. Does that sound familiar?"

But no one was coming to mind for Jay, and so we moved on.

I shared several messages with the other attendants. We were just about to close the session when Jay sat bolt upright. "I know!" he exclaimed. "I've got so many friends on the other side now that I wasn't sure who you were talking about. But now I know them. They were my friends from Alcoholics Anonymous. It totally makes sense. We were all trying to save ourselves and each other from drowning in our addictions. We used to talk about AA as a lifeline."

"Like a real life Love Boat of support," I remarked.

"Yes. I've been asking them to come back for a while now. I wanted a sign that they're listening. Life is a long ride if you're in the boat alone, you know?"

"I do know. But they're angels now—your AA angels. They'll always be there when you need a little extra flotation!"

CHANNEL 5

Mothers Know Best

L ike fathers, mothers continue to love and watch over their children even after their earthly bodies are gone. Sometimes, they show up as guiding angels for their sons and daughters. At other times, they are fierce protectors, mama-managers keeping their children's to-do lists current. Even those who had challenging relationships with their children on Earth often circle back around as guiding lights.

Being with Bea

Bea Marx was an earth angel in her lifetime. Mother of three, devoted wife, soccer coach, cancer survivor of thirteen years, yoga instructor, Reiki master, spiritual inspirer... Bea wore many hats!

Her arrival at the Yoga Center in 2004 preceded a major shift in her life. Alongside her twenty-five year old son, she dove headfirst into the yoga teacher training program. She knew it would be a great marriage of body and mind, a way to link her physical and metaphysical pursuits. After graduation, she became a source of healing energy for others both at the Center and throughout our community. She started a cancer support group called Wellness Warriors, held private meditation and Reiki sessions, and fully developed her energy healing skills. She was a role model for anyone living with illness or the fear of illness, and her healing hands were available for anyone who entered the Center.

In the midst of all of this amazing work, Bea suffered from a number of critical health scares of her own—but she was an expert at just "Bea-ing" in the moment, no matter what. Even as her body slipped into its final decline, she remained selfless, inspiring thousands to participate in an event called Yoga On the Steps: Living Beyond Breast Cancer, in Philadelphia. It was a spectacular vision to see so many yoga enthusiasts on the steps of the Philadelphia Art Museum, where Rocky was inspired to succeed in an iconic battle of his own.

In May 2011, Bea transitioned to the other side, but she still visits her students often. She can be felt in every room at the Center. Clients speak about visits from her in their dreams and meditations. Each time one of her many relatives is present at a channeling session, she speaks to them in great detail about what's transpiring in their lives. Even from the other side, she is still teaching her family to cope with loss—and how to be open to new paths of healing and spirituality.

Through me, she often teases her family about how she worked for years to get them to come to the Center and experience yoga while she was alive, but now that she's passed on they're here all the time. "We come to be with Bea," they tell me. I can't help but understand.

During yoga classes and channeling sessions, she often stands right in front of her friends and relatives, and places her spirit hands upon them as if offering Reiki. She also points out potential students of Reiki, and inspires these individuals to awaken to the power of their own healing hands. Nine times out of ten, the person she chooses is already on the path to Reiki certification, or is thinking about starting training. They always appreciate this encouragement.

When Bea comes forward to be channeled for her family, she often mentions Valentine's Day, her wedding day, with many heart-based details. In one reading, she spoke to her husband's sister. "Ask him about the mess this morning in the kitchen," she said through me. "And then, tell him it was just a test, to see the relevance of the emotional edges. After all, you can't cry over spilled milk!"

The sister, having heard the details from Bea's husband only that afternoon, laughed in agreement.

During another session, Bea gifted her brother-in-law, James, with a golden halo. This golden shimmer represents true Christ consciousness and alignment with that particular aspect of the divine. I have only seen this shimmer around two people before. (Chris, whose story appeared in Channel 2, was one.) James's halo was shining so brightly that it lit up the whole room. Others present in the session felt a brightening of the energy field. When I explained what was happening, James wept in profound understanding. This gift was a response to many spiritual questions he'd been asking privately for years.

Bea always lets her family know that she sees their daily lives. Once, when her family was present, she talked about their dogs, and a lost button in the kitchen. The button had fallen off of a basket that the dog was trying to make his home. They'd scooped it up that morning and placed it on the kitchen counter. The reality was, the dog was bigger than the basket. "It's like trying to stuff unconditional love in a basket," Bea said through me. "It just won't fit. It's everywhere!"

An Abundance of Love

The first time I met Rita, I was coming off a long drive from New Jersey to Maine. Keith and I had been dating for a while, and we were heading north so I could meet his mother, who owned an antiques barn in Camden, Maine. I had just finished a particularly trying week at the corporate job I was working, and the thought of stepping into some backwoods haven of dust and clutter at the end of a long day on the road was enough to make me feel less than cherubic. (Okay, I was downright grumpy.) Still, I knew I had to be on my best behavior: this was my future mother-in-law we were talking about, after all.

The moment I stepped into that barn, my trepidation dissolved. The space was chock full of collectibles, but also overflowing with love and angelic presence. Some of this presence was literal: there were statues and paintings of angels everywhere, in a multitude of styles and sizes. And then, there was that indefinable quality of lightness that accompanied the woman herself.

Rita was an extra-large woman, but she moved around her shop as if she was dancing. An abundance of playfulness and creativity flowed from her. The moment our eyes met, I felt our soul connection. Not what a woman usually expects from her mother-in-law! We had other things in common as well: Rita is my middle name, and Rita's mother and I share a birthday. That day, she gifted me with a beautiful angel pin, which I wore sincerely for years. It was like we'd become instant sisters in an angelic sorority!

In Sanskrit, Rita (Reeta) means all-encompassing, immortal, universal. Certainly all of these applied to my mother-in-law. She could make anyone feel at home in her antiques barn, or in her house (which rivaled the barn for its collection of angels and knickknacks). She was a wonderfully present grandmother to my three children, and a guiding guru in my own life. When she passed, it left a huge void for the entire family—but, in her usual loving way, she provided my husband and me with a great opportunity to speak to our children about life, death, and spirits.

At the time of Rita's passing, my capacity for mediumship hadn't yet been made public. To help myself practice this art, I would host other channelers at the Yoga Center and, while they were presenting to the group, test my perceptions against theirs. When my family asked to attend a channeling session to see if Rita would come through, I agreed immediately. I was sure that there would be at least a small message, especially since the channeling would take place at the Yoga Center, a place which Rita supported. Several of her antique ceramic angels were even hanging on the walls.

The session came and went, and there was no message from Rita. My children, who were twelve and thirteen at the time, were devastated. I was rather disappointed myself, but as we drove home I explained that sometimes we have to be patient with spirits. They're not always available at the times we prefer. Or, they may choose alternative ways to let us know that they see us.

"Your grandmother has shown me her presence many times in our house," I told them, "Most especially through the ice machine in the fridge. You know how it keeps acting up? That's your Grandma."

I felt the truth of my own words sink in. Spiritual timing is its own entity, and separate from earthly time. The famous medium John Edwards tells a beautiful story about his mother in his book, *Crossing Over*. While he had already helped thousands make the connection with their own loved ones by the time his mother passed, he had to wait two years to receive a confirmed message from her through another medium. He writes about how it's hard—sometimes nearly impossible—to offer readings for family, because they are the people about whom we know the most, and therefore the people about whom we have the most entrenched feelings (positive or negative). Our preconceived notions can put up barriers to messaging.

For her own reasons, unknown to us, Rita declined to put in an appearance at the Center that night, but that didn't mean she wasn't around. As soon as I mentioned the refrigerator, the kids knew exactly what I was talking about. For years (since Rita passed, in fact) we'd been putting up with erratic behavior from the ice machine in our luxury fridge. We would have it repaired, but within hours it always shut down again—at least until Rita's relatives were in town. Then, ice cubes spontaneously appeared in the tray! While it was certainly convenient to have ice while guests were staying, the machine inevitably shut down once the family left. My kids thought it was the greatest magic trick ever. I took it as a directive from Rita to encourage more family reunions.

In life, Rita was a Cancer, born in July, and the watery nature of her sign perfectly suited her emotional character. On hot summer days, she would fill a glass with ice cubes, and drink glass after glass of icy water. If there was one thing in her kitchen to which Rita was attached, it was her ice maker. It only seemed fitting that she would tamper with ours.

As we drove home from the channeling session, I sensed that my kids were disappointed. I sent out a silent prayer. *Rita, please give us a sign! Let us know that you're there, and watching over your grandchildren! They are at a pivotal point, and asking great questions about the angelic realm. Help me know how to answer them!*

When we got home, my kids ran to the fridge. In the tray were five perfectly formed ice cubes—one for each member of our family.

"Mom!" My son breathed. "Did you do a magic trick?"

"No, sweetheart. But your grandmother did!"

*   *   *

Six years later, my daughter and I attended a channeling session in New York with a well-known psychic. The experience was a profound one for me, because it showed me that even though I was a full-fledged channeler myself by that point, I could still harbor doubts and judgments around spirit messaging.

This channeler brought Rita through for us immediately. She mentioned that my mother-in-law was with Bernie, her ex-husband. I was immediately skeptical. Rita held few grudges, but Bernie was always a sore spot. The mere mention of that relationship brought up huge amounts of pain for her. "There's no way she would be with him," I replied defiantly. "She couldn't stand him. No one in the family has spoken to him in twenty years! No, no, no—" I froze, and looked down at myself. My arms and legs were tightly crossed, and my brow crunchy. I was acting as resistant as some of my own clients! I hadn't heard what I wanted to hear, so I jumped into denial.

The channeler patiently supplied more details, until I couldn't help but acknowledge that my father-in-law was indeed present with Rita in Heaven. Once I got over the shock, I realized that there was no reason why Bernie and Rita shouldn't be together. Earthly anger doesn't apply on the other side of the veil, and forgiveness is both easy and natural in the other realms. Why shouldn't that be true for my angelic mother-in-law?

And more, why shouldn't it be true for me? For all of us?

A few more small messages came through in that session, but that lesson in forgiveness was the most important. We don't need to wait until we get to Heaven to forgive old wrongs. If Rita had been able to forgive Bernie in life, she wouldn't have had to carry all that hurt for so long. When we harbor emotional resentment, it takes up storage space in our bodies—space that could be filled with love.

My reaction to Rita's message showed me that I was carrying a little chunk of Rita's old resentment, tossing it around as judgment against Bernie and his actions in life. Apparently, it was time for a little forgiveness of my own!

Mary's Mom and the Never-Ending To-Do List

Mary has been a student and client at the Yoga Center for many years. She's always had an inquiring mind, and has tried every class, workshop, and therapy we offer, including yoga, Pilates, breath work, meditations, massage—and finally, channeled communication.

At first, I was surprised to see Mary at our group channeling session. She has a strong religious background, and I wasn't sure how my mediumship practices would sit with her. I needn't have worried: her openness has allowed her to become one of the most regularly communicated-to clients at the Center!

Mary's mother was always a strong presence in her life. She continued to be so even after death. Session after session, Mary's mom showed up with a to-do list for her daughter, encouraging her to mend fences and repair her wounded heart.

Here are Mary's reflections from her first group session.

Dear Alaine;

I was thrilled with the meditation session this evening for a few reasons.

As a young child, I heard relatives and friends tell stories about visitations from God and the spirits of priests and loved ones who had passed on. I remember telling my mother that I wished such an exciting event would happen to me. As I matured, I held on to that desire. Now, I'm fifty-five, and I've only caught glimpses of the spirit world twice in the last ten years—until last night, when I had "magic number three!"

I realize that my mind is shifting as I get older. I'm sure that I'm thinking more about death and what lies beyond this existence. I miss terribly the people who have meant so much to me over the years, and I'm always wondering where they've gone. After tonight's meditation, I feel better in so many ways. There is life after death, even if it isn't life as we know it here. It was a joy to hear the experiences of all the other souls in the room, and to hear from my mom again. Fear and anxiousness have been removed from my mind. I am fascinated by this new method of communication.

Mary's mom showed up consistently after that first session, always in her favorite apron with the embroidered strawberries on the pockets. She showed kitchen utensils quite often—utensils that her daughter had inherited.

After attending subsequent sessions over a period of a few months, Mary wrote the following:

I figure that my mom is showing up through you as the Soul Food Peacemaker! She died fifteen years ago and was very sick for the last eight years of her life. In her final two years, she began to teach my dad how to cook for himself, since she couldn't do it for him anymore. I would also host dinners for the whole family every weekend and on holidays, because I loved to cook as much as my mother did. I would always make a bit extra for my dad, so he wouldn't have to struggle over the stove for daily meals on his own.

After my mom's death, there was a terrible disagreement in the family that divided us for years. We stopped communicating altogether for a long time. About a month before I went to my first channeled meditation session at the Yoga Center, we began to re-engage in conversation, but it felt cold and forced. During that session, my mother showed up with her baking pans and told me that I needed to reach out to someone "in the neighborhood." I had no idea what she meant. Was she talking about an actual neighbor? Someone else who was close to me? She repeated the same message in the next session—and then I got it. I needed to stop helping my neighbors more than I was helping my father! It was my own stubbornness which was preventing this reunion. I reached out, more wholeheartedly this time, and started a real conversation with my dad.

In the next session, my mother came through with a fuller heart, still in her special apron. "You need to bring some food to your father," she scolded me. "It's a peace offering."

I have come to the conclusion that I must return to the task of looking after my father—not just for his sake, but for my mom's. In the last two weeks, my father and I have apologized to one another, and have started to move on. He is now eighty-seven, and has little time left to him on this planet.

My mother was the kindest person in the world, and always wanted everyone else to be happy. Through you, Alaine, she has been able to bring our family back together. She made it happen with these sessions! Thank

*you for sharing this gift with me and with everyone else
who attends your sessions!*

Mary's mom continued to show up with a "to-do" list for her daughter until Mary moved out of state and was no longer able to attend monthly group channeling sessions. Even from Heaven, Mom was doing her best to keep her family whole and happy—and most importantly, well-fed!

CHANNEL 6

Heaven Can Wait

*D*uring the guided meditation sessions, I've become a bit of a frequent flier to Heaven. Being at that altitude for hours at a time can leave me buzzing like a bee, and it can take a little while for my feet to land on the earth again. I am always careful to arrange my sessions so that I have time to re-integrate before business meetings or other activities where logic is needed. One time, I scheduled a business meeting immediately following a session; I agreed to every sales proposition possible!

Experientially, I understand the desire many people have to retreat to the heavenly realms. It's an inexpensive escape from our everyday drama, and pulls us back to what's important. I think this is one reason why meditation has become so popular in the Western world: we all have an innate need to return home to the arms of a loving Source.

Many people don't have the patience to sit still and access this state of universal consciousness. Others want to remain in that state forever—especially if they have loved ones residing there, in the afterlife. Being in a constant "halfway" state seems easier than living without their dear ones. They might wonder how much their own will matters when it comes to the Big D—departure. Frequently, these people are the ones who seek me out. They are floating on Heaven's borders, looking for a doorway through which to chat with their loved ones and receive their enlightened guidance.

This heavenly story begins with Adam. (No, his beloved's name wasn't Eve!) I'd met him months before at a crystal bowl concert we'd hosted at the Center. He was a tall, dignified man in his late seventies who moved with a good-natured swagger. I didn't think anyone could swagger at his age—but Adam, with his full head of silver hair and brilliant smile, did just that.

On the day he came in for his reading, along with two of his seven children, he looked nothing like the man I remembered from the concert. Instead of waltzing in with a grin, he leaned on the shoulders of his daughters, and looked pale and weak. I decided to wait to see what our session would bring up before I expressed my concern.

We meditated together, and Adam's beloved wife of fifty-five years, Mary, came through right away. We were immediately enveloped in a cocoon of angelic vibration. She spoke to her daughters first, and seemed to know every detail of their lives. I guess you can't raise a family of seven children without a great deal of efficiency! I could also feel the high level of emotional intelligence in the family.

Mary told me that Adam had been a celebrated cardiac surgeon before his retirement, but that he needed his own heart healing today. I was in awe of the love that poured from her spirit—like there was no distance at all between the two of them. No wonder they missed each other's touch, I thought.

"Adam," Mary said through me. "You will have to wait to attend Heaven. We can be together while you are still on Earth. It's not your time to relocate."

I knew that this was the purpose of our meeting. Adam, longing for his wife, was spending too much time seeking the heavenly realms instead of living here on Earth.

"Marcy and Karlene," Mary continued. "Thank you for coming with your father to this meeting. I love you both dearly. I know you think of me often, just as I think of you often. But I also know that your lives are here, fully. Karlene, you are going to move in with your father. You can help him with this understanding."

Karlene jumped in her seat. Apparently, this was the exact advice she'd been hoping to hear from her mom. "This is a purposeful change of residence," Mary confirmed. "You will be a caretaker for your father, but also for yourself."

Adam muttered something about being "plenty self-sufficient, thank you very much," but he was smiling. His beloved wife was still managing the family dynamic, just as she had for more than five decades.

"Karlene," Mary said, "You need to resolve your financial issues, and heal yourself after your gall bladder removal. You should remove caffeine and dairy from your diet immediately. You're a nurse: it's time to use your healing hands more energetically, for your patients and yourself. And of course, for your dad."

Karlene had been alternately giggling and dropping her jaw throughout this latest message. "I got my Reiki certification a little while ago. I've been practicing. And the other stuff, the debt and the diet, well—" she glanced at her father "—I'm working on it."

"You'll receive confirmation in the form of blue butterflies," I told her.

"Oh! Mom loved blue butterflies! They were her favorite!"

Now, it was Marcy's turn. "She sees your head as a brilliant crystal, illuminated. What about that symbolism resonates with you?"

"I just got back from Sedona, Arizona," Marcy told me in a slightly shaky voice. "I was in the presence of a famous Crystal Skull named Max."

"Wow," I breathed. I'd known I was looking at crystal energy, but I had never seen someone wearing it as a headpiece!

"There's also some relationship advice," I told her. "As a loving partner, it's not always the best approach to let your partner know that you're worried about him. We all want to be cared for, but worry disempowers men especially. Be trusting of his ability to work through his own challenges. Your confidence provides faith, but worry is fear."

Mary continued with more directives for both girls, including information about Adam's blood pressure medication and which doctors to stay with. All three were amazed that she could still be so involved in the day-to-day activities of their lives. Then, finally, she turned her attention to her husband.

"Your job on Earth isn't complete yet," she said through me. "It's not time for reunion. You are an elder, a teacher of transition with dignity. You can affirm your presence on the physical plane by taking up breathing practices, and setting up a meditation altar at the bayside window, the one that overlooks the birdhouse."

"That's already set up," Marcy said. "In my house. You can come over anytime, Dad."

"Put your stethoscope on the altar, Adam. It's a stunning symbol of the lives you've saved. Now, you have to save your own life. Heaven can wait."

Mary shared with me privately that Adam had been having episodes of fainting lately because he was confused about whether he should be here with his family or with her in the afterlife. One foot on Earth, the other in Heaven. That's why he'd seemed so weak and transparent when he came in for the reading.

"You need to share your brownie story with him," she told me. I nodded.

"Mary wants me to share this story with you," I said aloud. "I used to have blackouts as well."

Adam looked up, surprised. Neither he nor his daughters had said anything about his fainting spells.

"I used to be a little naïve," I joked. "In 2004, I was under the impression that I was in complete control of my body. I'd been a vegetarian my whole life. I did triathlons. I was always training for what came next, and was critical and controlling of everything that went into my body.

"One day, I stopped by the health food store for a vegan brownie. When I opened the package, I saw that it was sprinkled with confectioner's sugar. It felt so decadent to eat it! But later that night, I discovered that what I thought was a fresh brownie was, in fact, expired—and that white stuff wasn't sugar. It was mold!

"Once I got to the emergency room, the doctors figured out what was wrong with me pretty quickly: I'd had a severe allergic reaction. They didn't keep me long at the hospital, but they did warn me that I was in for a lengthy recovery—and they were right. My fainting spells could appear at any time of day, anywhere. I was NOT in control of my body. I was afraid all the time. It got to the point where it was easier to be blacked out, just so I could be away from the fear of blacking out. I had to learn the art of surrender."

I turned to Adam. "I think Mary wanted you to hear that because you have always taken such impeccable care of yourself. You know what it takes to stay healthy in mind, heart, and spirit. You have a strong will to live. But right now, you're questioning that. Staying here with your family isn't as easy as taking your joy rides to Heaven. She wants me to remind you that there's still plenty of love and adventure here on Earth."

"So my fainting spells are like your brownie episode?" he asked.

"I think so. And you know what? Every year on my birthday, my girlfriends bake me a brownie cake with confectioner's sugar on top, just in case I get too scared again. Sometimes, you just have to laugh at life, and jump back into it with both feet."

"I don't know," he admitted. "Sometimes I think about how many more lives I could have saved, when I was a cardiologist. There was always something more I could have done. When Mary was here, I knew it was all alright—but now, I'm not sure I belong here anymore."

"I think that's why she wants you to put the stethoscope on your meditation altar. Think about what you accomplished, and how many lives you saved. This is like nutrition for your heart. You extended so many lives. It will be empowering for you to do this for yourself."

"You know, you're right. Or rather, Mary is right. She always was." He grinned, and stood up unassisted. He looked like a new man, with lively color in his face and a perfectly straight back. His daughters beamed at him. He approached me, pulled me to my feet, and enveloped me in a gentle hug. I felt his heart against mine, and knew how healthy this man truly was. I didn't want to let him go. I'd looked at love from both sides, and become the channel and mirror for a profound healing. It was akin to performing spiritual surgery.

"Heaven can wait," I said again, quietly, as Adam and his daughters walked out of the room.

A week or so later, Marcy sent me a letter, confirming that Adam's "surgery" had been successful.

My Dear Alaine,

What is a lifetime of love when one is left behind? Are seven children enough of a reminder of a mother's love, a love so great that she still finds a way to get through to us? All of her messages were those of love and comfort, and promises of nothing but greatness on the other side of the veil. No time or space separates my mother from my father; it all seems so current. Their hearts are still entwined as one. I think that she made the choice to stay connected to him beyond this life.

You are absolutely correct that the man who walked into your studio was not the same man who walked out. The gift you gave us was one of comfort, peace, and overwhelming love. What more could one wish for? You are truly amazing, and I am so grateful that you are sharing your gifts in a way that heals so many people.

Much love,

Marcy

Heaven Couldn't Wait... And Neither Could He

Before I start my group channeling sessions, I invite each person to say hello, and ask whether they have ever attended a session like this before. On this particular evening, one woman became visibly nervous.

"My name is May, and I have been here for a session once before." She started to shake, and reached for the box of tissues a few feet away. "Last time I was here, you told me that I had a spirit named Frank around me. The only Frank I knew was my daughter's ex-boyfriend. She's older now, and doesn't live with me anymore. We don't even talk on the phone, only through text messages. As far as I knew, Frank was still alive, so I kind of brushed off the message.

"When I got in my car after that session was over, I saw that my daughter had actually called me. I called her back, and she said that she'd just learned that Frank—her ex—had committed suicide the day before. I started screaming. I was a nervous wreck all the way home."

The room was silent. I was caught off-guard myself. I realized that I was hosting immediately departed souls, something that had never happened before.

"I'm so sorry," I told her. "It's not often that a spirit shows up to communicate so close to his transition."

"It's okay," she said, wiping her eyes. "I came back tonight because this whole thing actually helped me reconnect with my daughter. It opened the door for us to talk about Heaven, and share our beliefs. It's common ground."

We started the meditation, and Frank came through for May again. She recognized him by newer details, like the song that was special for him and her daughter. The lyrics were also part of the eulogy May's daughter delivered at Frank's funeral.

"Antidepressants have another side to them," Frank told May through me. "I congratulate your daughter for having the strength to lessen her own anxiety and depression through natural means. I support you both in your relationship, and encourage you to create more attachment and closeness there. She won't acknowledge it yet, but she needs you in her life."

It was an impactful message for everyone. I was so grateful to May for coming back to share her experience, and Frank's wisdom, with our group.

After our session, I discovered that I had a message of my own on my cell phone. A client had called me to say that the grandchildren I'd seen around her in our last reading were coming through into the world: her son and his wife were expecting their first child! It was certainly a lighter prediction than the one which had initially come through around Frank, but also confirmed for me that both arrivals and departures can be equally blessed and beautiful.

Cellular Connections

Natalie, having heard that I offer spiritual counseling of the channeled sort, called me directly on my cell phone to request an appointment for herself and her family. When I asked when they wanted to come in, her answer was, "Immediately!" Natalie wanted to bring her mother to visit with her dearly departed husband, Rudy (Natalie's father). While we were working out the soonest available time over our crackly Bluetooth connection, I spontaneously downloaded the father's energy, right there in my car! Rarely does it happen that quickly for me, and without the sitter present. I was intrigued that this father's spirit had bridged the boundaries I usually set around appointment times.

I shared this with Natalie. "He's asking for someone whose name starts with "C" to come with you, too. Who is he talking about?"

Natalie was silent for a moment. "Carol is my aunt. Dad's sister. This is beyond coincidence; I've been trying to get in touch with her all day. She was just diagnosed with breast cancer—the same kind I was just re-diagnosed with after nineteen years in remission."

The connection was uncanny. And although Aunt Carol wasn't available for the reading, Natalie's sister Julie was able to attend in support of their mother.

Rudy's spirit stayed with me for the remainder of my road trip, buzzing nervously about his upcoming family reunion. I tried to breathe deeply and stay calm. It's always an honor to be a bridge for a loving family, but I needed to keep my eyes on the road!

Within minutes of my arrival at the Yoga Center, Natalie and her family were ready to get started. Rudy came through immediately, and called out for Randy.

"Who's Randy?" I asked.

"Our brother," Natalie told me. "Dad's only son. They were so close."

"I feel like he's taking roll call of the entire family!"

Natalie nodded. "Dad would do that."

Next, Rudy turned his attention to his wife. "My love," he said through me, "Let go of your guilt. Don't blame yourself for not reacting sooner to my discomfort, or not getting me to the hospital more quickly. It was my time to go. My heart would have given out anyway. Nothing you did would have changed that. Worrying about it is a waste of time."

Natalie's mother wept as she released her guilt over her husband's heart attack. When she was calmer, Rudy continued. "Let loose, darling. Don't bind yourself up in me. Be of healthy mind and spirit for our daughters. They need and want you here to support them."

Later, Natalie wrote to me.

Dear Alaine,

We all felt very good about the session. I believe you really helped my mother, and I hope that she stays in the positive state she was in when she walked away from our session. It was very interesting and helpful for me to hear what my father wanted to share with us as well. His messages brought us peace and understanding about how to move forward in a kind, gentle, loving way.

On Father's Day, we went to Dad's grave. I could see the change in my mother and my brother, Randy. We're all slowly realizing that Dad's spirit is not exclusively preserved in the grave. He can be in many locations, wherever we may roam. Mom seems to have a different perspective on my father's passing now. She's expanding their relationship to bring a little more Heaven into our lives here on Earth. It's fueling a sense of security and protection versus fear and separation. It's a much healthier balance.

Kindly,

Natalie

Chad's Constant Contact

Becky, a local elementary school teacher, came to a group session at the Center just a short time before her world turned upside-down. She received some general messaging, and left deeply intrigued.

One morning a few weeks later, her husband Chad woke gasping and choking. Becky immediately called 9-1-1 and administered CPR, but that brought only temporary relief. Chad passed away in the hospital. He was just forty-one.

This propelled Becky into unknown territory. Overnight, she became the single mom of two children, and fell into a state of financial chaos. Both she and Chad had been actively involved in several charitable causes; now, she found herself in need of the same assistance she had once provided.

Not long after Chad passed, she requested another session with me. She still felt his presence every day, and wanted an unbiased mediator to make sure she wasn't "seeing things."

Chad was very talkative, just as he had been in life. He apologized profusely for the mess he'd left for his beloved wife, and added personal loving messages to remind Becky of her great strength. "Don't give up, honey," he said through me. "We'll be together again soon enough. Your place right now is clearly with our kids, and the kids you teach every day—but you don't need to get an 'A' in grieving. Take as much time as you need to heal this."

Becky laughed through her tears. "I was feeling pressure to be okay, and move on quickly," she shared. "I want to be on the other side of this, for my kids' sake."

"You'll get there," I promised.

A few months later, she returned again. Chad was available as soon as Becky arrived. He spoke with uncanny precision about their kids, providing specific instructions about their daughter's birthday cake and how he wanted it decorated.

"Why would a father dictate details about flowers and colors on a cake?" I asked Becky. "That doesn't seem typical at all."

"He made every one of her birthday cakes for the last thirteen years," she said. "He loved to bake for us."

Timidly, Becky asked, "Could the kids come to our next session?"

"Of course!" I knew it would be a beautiful thing for these kids to experience their father's love from beyond the veil. We set the date and Becky left the Center smiling.

For this third session, Chad was once again ready the moment his family arrived. His daughter could feel his presence right away, and said so. Her younger brother, however, was only experiencing his dad's absence—until Chad mentioned the family trip to Washington which had just been scheduled.

"Dad's coming on vacation with us?" he asked. "Cool!"

Other messages came through, about report cards and sports and how the kids should spend their summer. When everything had been said, I asked the kids, "What's your perspective on Heaven? Can it wait?"

Chad's son immediately said, "Yes. I want to visit Heaven, but I want to come back. I think it's a really peaceful place, with lots of fresh water. But I'm too young to go there forever. I want to be here. I want to live."

The daughter said, "It's funny. Heaven is everywhere to me. I feel Dad tugging on my hair when I'm in school, just the way he used to. He's here all the time, so I know Heaven is here too. But Heaven... That's where I'll go when I get old and bored with my life here on

Earth. I'm not ready to go there yet, except to visit Dad every once in a while."

Becky and I exchanged a knowing glance. From the mouths of babes...

A Note from Kara

Kara is a client who visits the Center regularly. She has an impressive knack for spiritual connection, and invites the presence of what lies beyond into her everyday life. We've traveled together to many sacred places: Sedona, Machu Picchu, and Lake Titicaca, to name a few. No matter where she's located, Kara has the power to bring Heaven down to Earth. Her presence at the Center consistently helps others lift their consciousness.

Kara reaches out to her deceased husband quite often. This brief letter is one she wrote to me after the first time I channeled her husband's spirit publicly.

Dear Alaine,

My husband and I talked about being able to connect after death many times during our years together, so it was no surprise that, within minutes of his passing, he let me know all was well with him. Since then, he has communicated quite often. I keep a journal of his visits so I'll never forget them.

An unexpected visit occurred when I was trying to be of support to you during one of your public sessions. My husband introduced himself to the group with a nickname that his business partner had given him years ago. It took me completely off guard; up until then, he'd only communicated privately.

It is so comforting to know that our spirits can continue to 'be' on another plane of existence. These experiences in connection have removed all fear of death from me. I'm so grateful to you for sharing them with me, and with others.

Blessings of Peace and Love,

Kara

CHANNEL 7

Tuning In

Since I started offering channeling sessions around the globe, I've communicated thousands of messages from departed loved ones to the friends and family members who've sought me out as a conduit. I've also fielded multiple questions about my abilities as a medium and how my "powers" work. But near or far, foreign or domestic, the most common question is, "When did you know that you could see and hear spirits?"

I discovered my unique ability when I was very young. It began as a strong, intuitive sixth sense that I was able, with a little concentration, to sharpen and enhance. When I was six years old, our family visited a National Park near Lake Placid, New York. I was swept away by the enormity and wisdom of the forest. I wandered away from my parents to converse with the pines and spruces. I experienced the ancient trees as glorious natural record-keepers.

Distracted by this exchange, I completely lost sight of my family. I was blazing my own trail, hearing the trees call my name, "Alaine! ALAINE!" In response, I would sprint over to the tree that had summoned me, and throw my arms around it. I remember wondering who else could hear the alien voices of the forest—a resonance infused with the strength of earth and wind. It was like no other sound I'd ever encountered.

After greeting a few trees, I asked aloud, "Who's calling me?" I was told, simply, "Spirit!" I couldn't believe I'd gotten an answer! Even though I didn't understand the enormity of what I was experiencing, I knew that I had received a direct, decisive, totally non-human reply to my question. The tree-voices continued to call my name, and I touched them one by one. The day took on a "birthday" feeling: this was *my* day, and it was special in a way that no other day could be. I was embarking on a treasure hunt of joy and discovery.

Eventually, I settled down at the foot of a particularly inviting giant, curling up in the hollow between two enormous roots. I felt coddled, cocooned, totally protected—like I was with my original "extended family." I may have fallen asleep for a little while.

And then, I was jolted back to the reality of my six-year-old self by my agitated parents and a harried-looking park ranger. I heard the tale of a frantic thirty-minute search for a lost child. I wanted to ignore them. I felt more at home with my new family of tree spirits than I did with my human parents, who were always sparring. There were no gentle branches, olive or otherwise, offered in my family!

"I wasn't lost," I told them indignantly. "I was right here all along."

My mother reached down to pull me to my feet. "Come on, Alaine. It's time to go."

But I wouldn't budge. I couldn't leave this mystical tree, with its soft, soothing voice. I couldn't leave this forest where I'd been so warmly, unconditionally received. The more insistent my parents became, the more determined I was to stay put. Couldn't they hear the trees? Couldn't they see that life was vibrant here in this forest, so much more than it could ever be at home?

Since I couldn't make my parents disappear, I resorted to my next best tactic: an all-out temper tantrum. My parents were mortified. They threatened to leave me alone again—but this motivated me even more. I wanted them to go!

"Tell her the park is closing," my mother begged the ranger. "Tell her we have to go, now!"

"Come on, kiddo," the ranger said. "Your mom is right. It's time to go." But I saw the twinkle in her eye, and I was sure she knew exactly where I was coming from.

That was a defining day for me. I learned that I had the ability to hear voices that others couldn't. I learned that I could communicate with beings beyond the scope of ordinary perception. I learned that nature walks, and talks, endlessly. The volume on my spiritual channel was turned up to "maximum," and I was ready to listen.

You've Got the Power!

Another question to which many students are "dying" to know the answer (no pun intended) is, "Can I connect with my departed loved ones on my own, without the intercession of a medium?"

The answer, of course, is yes.

Inhabiting the often surprising land of spiritual communication and symbolic language, I've wondered if what I do can be taught. For a long time, while I was learning to embrace my gift rather than run from it, I figured I was just a freak of nature, a psychic anomaly. But since I've stepped up to take full ownership of my skills as a spiritual communicator, I've learned that everyone—regardless of age, gender, religious background, ethnicity, or education—can learn to receive messages from Heaven and its residents about their own lives. There's no such thing as spiritual deafness.

When we are appropriately attuned, we can make endless discoveries about ourselves and our place in this world. These truths come from within, but are reflected back at us by other people, energies, or objects. When we're willing to look, we can find profound understanding in these reflections. There are endless possibilities for symbolic responses to your personal spiritual questions.

As a medium, I am a mirror. I reflect the communications of spirit guides back to those who are ready to receive their messages. I am not the source of the messages, only the tool by which they are delivered. With practice, I've been able to fine-tune my spiritual perception. In each reading, I might utilize visions, sounds, smells, physical sensations, and spoken words to translate the "spiritual code" of the messages I receive. This is a unique style that works for my personality and the intention I hold in my communication.

Other rituals have helped as well. I feel that being a lifelong vegetarian has enabled me to clear any energetic "fog" from my mirror, so that what is reflected is as pure as possible. Yoga and meditation help keep my body free from discomfort, and my mind free of useless chatter and clutter. If I didn't care for my body and mind in these ways, I believe my spiritual outreach to others would be compromised.

My daily practices are vital to keeping my level of attunement, but other practitioners follow their own recipes for success. My friend April, a healer located in the Florida Keys, swims with dolphins almost daily. Another healer, Rick, meditates in the morning before he heads off to his day job as the manager of an off-track betting hall. During his hour-long commute, he "talks to the pines, and listens for the answers." Each individual has a unique way of plugging in for recharge.

Once the balance of mind and body has been established, you can begin the process of surrendering. Ultimately, the act of surrender is what allows altered states of consciousness to be achieved. Your intuition can be increased by spending quiet time in contemplation. Breathe deeply and evenly. Listen to your own thoughts, and then get out of the way to let the deeper truths come through. Once your "I" self—your ego—feels comfortable stepping out of the limelight for a few minutes, the most direct pathways to your heart will be revealed. From your heart, you can travel south to your gut, where instinct and intuition reside.

Listen to the messages that bubble up inside. I think of the hairs on my arms as spiritual antennae: when someone tells me a story that gives me "truth bumps" and makes my arm hair stand up, I know there's a powerful energy around us. When you sense a presence in the room, try to "see" its source without the filters of your logical mind. Trust your instinct and the messages it sends you, even if those messages seem fantastic at first.

A friend of mine taught himself to channel in order to grow his skill as a musician. His personal brand of spiritual communication is much different than mine. Here's what he wrote about cultivating his incredible aptitude for channeling famous drummers.

When I decided to teach myself how to play the drums, I would listen over and over to my favorite songs and try to copy the drum patterns I heard. In other words, I set out to copy the best drummers in the world, hit for hit, right from the start.

I noticed early on that each drummer had his (or her) own unique style of playing. Tone, timing, and nuance all went into creating a signature technique. The first step in learning to play like them was to listen to each note and try to process the sound I was hearing. What piece of the drum kit was producing that sound? How could I mimic that sound exactly in each instance it occurred? It was a lot like learning the letters of an entirely new alphabet. I needed this information in order to be able to "read" what was written in each of my favorite songs. Each note was part of a phrase, which was part of a rhythm, which was part of the whole piece of music.

As it turned out, learning the notes was the easy part. The tricky thing was putting it together in real time, where a delay of a fraction of a second can throw the whole song off-kilter. I found myself getting frustrated. My analytical approach was teaching me a lot, but it couldn't help me "feel" the music the way its creators had felt it.

It was at this point that I started channeling.

For me, "channeling" means something different than it means for other people. It's the ability to translate a sound entering my ear, process it in my mind, and send a signal out to my arms, legs, fingers, and feet—all in real time simultaneous to the music. I realized that this was exactly what needed to happen if I was going to play along with my favorite drummers. At first, it seemed daunting, even unachievable. But it became a real process once I got out of my own way and just allowed it to happen.

In the ear, through the brain, and out through the extremities in real time allows me to play "with the band." As my skills have increased, I've played side by side with some of the best drummers in history. Frankly, I don't care anymore if I miss a couple of notes here and there: it's about the music, and rock'n'roll ain't meant to be perfect!

Twenty Questions

Often, when new people come to a meditation session, they have a lot of fears and concerns about the "right and wrong" of a communicative connection to those who have passed over. If you have desired a relationship with a spirit guide, you may have asked yourself some of these questions as well.

Below are twenty of the most common queries about connecting with the realm of spirit.

#1: Are there evil spirits, and can they harm me?

I have never met a spirit who wasn't worth channeling. Of course, there are troubled spirits, just as there are troubled people in the world of the living—but like humans, spirits are generally in a learning process. Regardless of where they are in their own processes, these sprits can still offer helpful and healing messages to their loved ones.

While I've never experienced anything like a Hollywood-style haunting, discernment is key when it comes to screening messages. We need to be able to recognize whether a message is in alignment with our intentions. If a spirit's purpose is not serving the highest good, I don't allow him or her a guest pass, period.

#2: Have you ever channeled a spirit from Hell?

My belief system doesn't include the typical ideas of Heaven and Hell, and even with challenging messaging I always find a light switch. So when I'm asked if I can draw on dark energies, my answer is, emphatically, NO. The spirits I reflect (again, with discernment) are those who have transitioned. They've dropped their physical bodies off at the earthly depot, and angelic ways have overtaken any darker human tendencies.

#3: Have you ever gotten a message you didn't like?

When I'm communicating channeled messages, I'm very conscious that the sitter is able to hear the messages of love. Sometimes the sitter's defensiveness is intense, and I need to hold back the spirit's desire to share. The diversity in readings is extremely personal based on circumstance, the sitter, the spirit, and me (in that order). Whatever happens in a reading, I always trust that it is for the highest good.

And then, there was Rachel.

A thirty-something spiritual seeker, Rachel was highly intrigued by the channeling process—maybe even more than she was by the message. After a few attempts in a group setting, it was clear that she wasn't fully receiving the guidance I was offering. It was frustrating for me, so I offered her a complimentary private reading.

The information which surfaced from the private reading was accurate historically, but difficult for Rachel to accept emotionally. She cried and cried, filled with shadows of self-doubt which led her to believe that she couldn't be read by anyone. Although I had clearly seen and heard the spirit who was trying to communicate with her, I apologized profusely, and told her that I felt inadequate in this process. I referred her to another colleague, grabbed the remote, and changed the channel.

Another woman, Helen, came to me with her husband, who she claimed was there to support her "to the best of his ability." I wasn't convinced. Helen's father came through immediately, but I kept feeling like he was withholding information. It's really rare for that to happen, and it made me curious. After an hour of half-hearted messaging, Helen's father told me privately that he was dissatisfied and that Helen should come back for another reading.

Shocked, I conveyed the message. I told her that I would be happy to give her a second, complimentary session—but inside, I was a little disturbed that this spirit expected me to work overtime. It was more than presumptuous. I felt like a ventriloquist's dummy! Still, having felt the diminished voltage of Helen's father's messaging, I was intrigued (and a little nosy).

A few weeks passed before I finally heard from Helen. "I'm coming alone this time," she told me. I could practically feel her father smiling. Of course! He'd wanted to meet with his daughter alone. That was why he'd insisted I offer a buy-one-get-one!

Our second session was a beautiful, carefree reading. It was clear that Dad wasn't saying anything Helen's partner couldn't hear; he had simply wanted his daughter's undivided attention! It's amazing to me how spirits orchestrate circumstance.

#4: Do spirits inhabit your body when you channel them, like in the movies?

Not often, and when they do, it's momentary. Some mediums practice this way, but I prefer to keep my body to myself! This allows me to deliver messages without taking on the energy of the spirit being channeled.

That said, there are some spirits who "hitchhike." (David, from Channel 1, was one of these.) They don't intrude on my physical space, but hitch themselves loosely to me, like balloons tied to a car antenna. I feel them like a dream that stays with me throughout the day. Sometimes, they take me out of my physical space a bit—like personal angelic chauffeurs—but I never offer these hitchers a lift unless I sense that it's aligned with the universal high road.

#5: Can you feel trauma when someone died in pain?

Yes, if it's relevant to the message.

Once, early on in my channeling practice, a woman came to me to ask if she should adopt a baby girl. The birth mother had passed, and my sitter figured I could ask Mom if this adoption was okay with her.

When I opened myself to the spiritual connection, I started choking uncontrollably. It got so bad that I had to ask the client, "Why am I strangling? Did the baby's mother struggle at her time of death?"

Shocked, the client replied that yes, the mother had been strangled to death. Once recognition had been achieved, the spirit let me go, and I could breathe again. It was a powerful messaging, and the client did receive the blessing of the baby's mother for the adoption—but since then, I have protected myself better when spirits come into my field.

#6: Why do animals always show up in your sessions?

Personally, I don't see a difference between humans who act like animals and animals who act like humans! Like Obie from Channel 3, pets often present themselves to give comfort and joy to their owners. They also appear as confirmation that the sitter's loved ones are with them on the other side. Finally, animals' spirits embody unconditional love and joy no matter which side of the veil they're on. Their emotions are less complicated and tangled than those of their human owners. Sometimes, we just need to remember how simple loving communication can be!

#7: Do the spirits of the departed stay close to their families and friends?

It appears to be so with most soul families, regardless of time and earthly relationship. Every spirit's story is as unique as they are.

Some of those who have not left Earth permanently remain because their exit was sudden or premature, and their hearts are still with those who survived them. Others stay because they are still exchanging karmic lessons with friends, family, or rivals among the living. For those in this second space, remaining karma can often be resolved through channeled messaging. You can actually witness the energy exchange when someone is ready to release grief, greed, or guilt. Masters, guides, and relatives come through as their elevated selves, without their heavy, human footprints, and actively encourage freedom from negativity.

#8: Why do you talk about angels and gods in your readings?

Jesus, Buddha, Mother Teresa, Martin Luther King, saints, Archangels, ancestors, ascended masters, Elvis Presley. Whoever you're praying to is drawn into your energy field! Unlike us humans, spirits (especially the really powerful ones) can watch over many, many people at the same time. It's a reminder that your thoughts have the power to create your reality!

#9: Why do you see colors when you're channeling?

Spectrums of color are part of the language I use to interpret energetic fields, or auras. When we sit together in groups, there are opportunities to see one color or a mosaic.

Of course, when I mention colors, people's curiosity is piqued. What is the symbolic definition of this color, or that? My answer is always, "I don't know. I have a few suggestions for you, though!" This is because everyone has their own color wheel, and the significance of a color is different for every sitter.

#10: How can I get a spirit to show up for a second reading, or a third?

The answer is, you can't. No one can force a spirit to show him- or herself during a reading. It's all about the messages that want to be shared. Having a loved one's spirit show up for you over and over isn't a sign of success. There's no competition in spirituality!

#11: Have you ever received a message in a group reading that was for you and not anyone in the group?

One year into my public offerings, I had a spirit guide who showed up as "Jack." He looked exactly like my father's deceased best friend, but I never thought he was there for me. I thought he was a symbolic character to describe for someone else, or that I was supposed to use his name to reach out to someone else in the group. After two hours, though, nobody related to Jack. It was the first time I'd ever had a leftover spirit in a group reading.

"I guess you're unclaimed freight, Jack," I said, and felt him grin.

Jack was always jolly, a "kidder." His daughter was a childhood best friend of mine, but life had made us distant, and I hadn't talked to her in more than three decades. I took Jack's presence as a message to break our silence.

A Google search revealed that she'd gone to Harvard Medical School, and was an expert in the field of gynecology and women's issues. Would this successful, apparently very busy woman really want to hear from me about her recently fallen father reappearing? I decided to wait in the "patience office" for a while, to see what other messages came through.

Three days later, I got a call from Florida, where my father lived. He had been rushed to the hospital from his nursing home. The nurse indicated that he was transitioning rapidly. He passed on only moments after my plane touched down.

It wasn't until weeks later that I remembered Jack's visit. He hadn't shown up for me, or even for his daughter: he was telling me that he was waiting for my father, Hank, who he'd always called "Hanky Panky." It would be entirely in character for the two of them to wait for one another on the other side. They'd been inseparable in life—why not in the afterlife?

Since then, I've never had another personal guide show up in a group reading. They always book private appointments, so they can claim my full attention.

#12: Have you ever heard from a spirit that your sitter didn't know?

It happens surprisingly often! I never doubt these "session crashers," even if the sitters do. Relationships between soul families are always evolving, and our ancestors often watch over us even if we never had any interaction with them on the physical plane. The past can teach us volumes about the present, and when a spirit guide wants to get a message through, they do!

#13: What if someone has forgotten most of their childhood because of trauma, but a parent shows ups for messaging?

The message is always more important than the messenger. The guidance that comes through in a reading is intended to be loving and helpful, no matter its source. Sometimes, when trauma is a factor, having a friend or family member present at the reading can help validate messaging when the sitter is unable.

Two half-sisters came to me for a private reading. They were in their late forties, and had started researching their personal history together. I was concerned because Paige, the younger daughter, was resistant to responding. She didn't want her father to show up, but he did. The older sister, Lisa, knew much more information about his life than Paige did, and she was able to validate the images that I received more gracefully. Their dad came through with his head in a TV, like a living picture tube. It was an image that both sisters instantly accepted. The father was a brilliant engineer for many years, but became depressed when he lost his job and was forced to become a television salesman to support his family. Boredom was a death sentence to this man, so he set sparks flying with regular arguments.

No sooner did we greet Dad than the stereo short-circuited in the room! The stereo screen warned us in bright red lights, "protect, protect!" I had never seen that particular warning before. At that point, I knew there were fragile emotional layers to unwrap here.

Paige was told by a healer prior to our sitting that she endured mental and perhaps physical trauma at her father's hands. She had blocked this out, but was working toward remembering and healing. She didn't want her father's presence to interfere with her healing process; she never wanted to hear from him again.

Lisa shared that her father was despised by many in the family for his violence, but that it took her mother ten long years to finally divorce him. Because Lisa was more open to receive his messages, Dad was able to explain his behaviors; he did not apologize, but it was clear he was trying to create another level of father-daughter relationship possibility.

#14: Why do spirits mention their final moments so often in readings?

Holding someone's hand during the final moments of their life on this earth creates a powerful bond. Spirits who have transitioned this way express their gratitude to the ones who sat with them during their passing. Even if a relationship was volatile while a person was alive, a transition experienced in this way can be healing for both parties. Its heart-to-heart hand holding!

Spirits also love to talk about their own funerals! The funeral is usually the most recent memory a sitter will have of the deceased, and because it proves that the spirit has been watching his or her loved ones, even from the other side of the veil.

#15: Can spirits move objects in my house, knock things over, or see my messy kitchen and closets?

The short answer is, yes! The spirits of those you love are likely to try to connect with you in your living space. Sometimes, when you get home to find that your favorite vase has been moved from one end of the table to the other, or a painting has been knocked off the wall, it's because a spirit is trying to get your attention. (And yes, clumsy people make clumsy spirits—otherwise, how would you recognize them?)

Spirits may also mention things around your home to let you know that they've been keeping an eye on you. Remember Mike, from Channel 3? His father showed up in a session to tell Mike to move his favorite picture out of the spare bedroom and put it somewhere where his handsome face could be seen more often!

#16: Can spirits find you when you're not at home or in a sacred space?

Of course! As long as your spiritual antennae are tuned in to the "open" channel, you can receive messages from spirits wherever you are. You'll notice, of course, that you feel more open and available in certain places. (I wouldn't try to channel on a New York subway train, myself!) Turn down the distraction of cell phones, headphones, television, gossip, worries, etc. In time, you may find that you seek out one particular place as your spiritual "call center!"

#17: Do deceased beloveds see our current relationships?

Yes! And usually, they're happy if you are! About fifteen of us were in a semi-private session in Florida, when one spirit, Michael, raced into the room on his motorcycle. He found his lover immediately, and threw a bucket of red hearts at her feet! I could feel the romance of this reunion. He had so much love to offer, it was literally pouring out into the room.

When I told Leslie, his beloved, what was happening, she shrieked. "Oh, my God! Michael was my first husband. He died in a motorcycle accident!" She was overwhelmed by the message of his love. He thanked her for all of the love that she gave to him, and told her how happy he was that she was in a healthy second marriage and that their son was thriving. He mentioned a piece of jewelry, a ruby. Tearfully, Leslie shared that Michael passed away only ten days before the birth of their son. Two weeks later, a jewelry store called to ask if Michael was going to come and pick up the ruby heart earrings he'd ordered for Leslie for their anniversary. She still wears those earrings today as a symbol of their everlasting love.

There wasn't a dry eye in the room as this romantic love story unfolded. All these years later, "Archangel Michael" was still throwing ruby hearts at the feet of his eternal beloved!

#18: Do you ever have to turn your channeling off?

At first, when I was still getting familiar with my channeling practice, I left my office door open all the time. Spirits showed up in my house, at the Jersey Shore, at the Yoga Center during classes, while I was in the shower... But it wasn't until I took a student completely by surprise with a channeled message that I realized that I needed to put a "Closed" sign on my door more frequently. After a weeknight yoga class, I approached a student to share the channeled message I'd received while the class was in Śavasana. She was shocked, and entirely unprepared to receive the communication. It wasn't that she was opposed to what I had to say, but it felt like an intrusion rather than a gift. After that, I decided to only transmit messages when I have the full permission of the recipient.

#19: Do you ever receive messages from spirits who don't speak English?

Of course! Rather than in words, these spirits speak to me through symbols and feelings. There are practicing mediums who can pull words through the veil, and speak to their clients in languages they themselves don't understand in their daily lives—but that's not how things work for me. If I have trouble understanding the symbolism a spirit presents, the spirit will often bring in a friend or loved one who can act as a translator for me.

This cooperative effort between spirits has happened several times, over sight and overseas!

#20: Do you ever see objects or images from someone's past (or past lives)?

I often receive such images if a person's past is related to a particular religion or culture (or both). Here's a good example a client shared with me in a letter:

Dear Alaine,

My name is Polly, and I want to thank you for coming to our studio yesterday and doing the guided meditation with us. It was truly an amazing experience, and I'm still at the beginning of trying to process all of it. Thank you for jumpstarting my energetic juices!

Yesterday you saw a totem pole behind me. I was shocked and greatly moved by this. It wasn't what I was expecting. I guess I thought you'd see my long-gone grandparents, or all of my dear departed pets. But the totem pole was hugely significant for me. I have always felt a deep connection to the Native American culture. I'm drawn to it: it's magnetic. Sometimes I have a feeling of "knowing" I've seen this place or that. I recognize clothing and smells that have never before appeared in my life. I love wearing turquoise and silver. I've been asked over and over if I have a Native American bloodline (which, by the way, I have not found any in our family genealogies).

I have only told a couple of people in my life about my belief that I was Native American in a past life. My sweet husband just grins and rolls his eyes at me. Last night when you saw a totem pole behind me, he smiled—but didn't roll his eyes this time!

Thank you again for walking onto my path!

CHANNEL 8

A Summer Summary

Ah, exhale...

I never thought of a true ending for this book. I don't believe in endings. I don't use words like "Goodbye." I can't even swat a fly, or eat a fish. To me, all life goes on, eternally.

Whatever personal messages of inspiration were delivered to you through these pages, they are eternal: they won't disease, die, or depart. You've explored the assumption that birth and death are absolute, rather than transitory states of being. You've asked the questions, "Is love everlasting?" "Who are my spirit guides?" Or maybe, "How can I let a tree RSVP?" These questions are gateways to a never-ending journey of self-realization. Let the stories in this book evoke your own absolute truths. Sometimes, we just need a little help to realize that we know what we know.

Writing this final chapter during the summer of 2013, I thought a lot about the act of asking for help. I deny myself that option often, for a few reasons. First, I'm pretty confident in my own self-sufficiency; help is something I give to others, not something I need for myself. Second, I trust that the solutions to my trials and tribulations will show themselves, so I save my favors for times of great need. Third, I harbor a teensy bit of fear that I'm not worthy of the help or guidance I'm asking for.

All of these excuses are foolish, of course. But I'm human, and a creature of habit. Still, I'm learning to expose my needs and ask for support when I need it. So, when I sat down to write this final chapter, I called in my spiritual SWAT team.

For the first couple of hours, I received only radio silence. I was beginning to think I would have to slog through the confusion of my human brain to complete this project on time. But then, I was offered this playful metaphor by none other than David, Judy's nephew, who emerged in one of the first stories in this compilation.

I felt a rising energy, like a labor pain. Then, my fingers wiggled on the keyboard. Here's what emerged.

A medium is a catalyst for potential energy shifting. An open channel gives spirit guides a voice. The position you play in the game of life is like that of a catcher at home base. You patiently await a play-by-play assignment for every batter (sitter) who gives permission to engage in dialogue, no matter what team they're assigned to— Team Life, or Team Afterlife. Any reunion with loved ones or God-Source is a home run for all!

"Wow! That's playful. I like that language!" I said aloud.

How did I know this came from David? Actually, I wasn't sure at first. I'm not a sports fan, so I knew this wasn't my metaphor; I would never compare Spirit to baseball! Even though the contact felt like his energy, I remained a bit skeptical. After all, I hadn't heard from his spirit in six months, and had no idea if he'd had an affinity for sports in life.

However, David *is* fond of orchestrating reunions, and supporting this book project (which I've jokingly called his "mini-biography") from the sidelines. When I felt his spirit come through, I'd forgotten that I was scheduled to have a Ya-Ya reunion just a few days later. Of course, his Aunt Judy was going to be there. Maybe, I thought, this metaphor wasn't just for me. Maybe it was a message for Judy as well.

Of course, I picked up the phone immediately.

"Did David have any connection to baseball?" I asked. I explained what had happened, and read her the message I'd typed.

"No," Judy replied. "I don't remember that he had a connection to any particular sport. Maybe he watched college football occasionally, but that was it. Maybe it wasn't him after all."

"Oh, okay. Thanks." I hung up, disappointed. Maybe my spiritual sense was on the fritz, I thought, because I'd been almost certain that it was David.

An hour later, Judy called me back. "Okay, I just talked to David's mom. The family just bought tickets to a baseball game. The match is between two teams that they always wanted to see square off against one another. It's happening at Wrigley Field, which is in the same town where David lived. That stadium has been on his dad's bucket list for years. The whole family is going to Chicago!"

"Wow! I guess the reference makes sense after all!"

"Plus, the annual charity race his family created is the weekend after the game. Remember when David wanted to design the tee shirts? He did! Everyone running for Team David is wearing shirts that say, 'Running is Stupid.' That was totally his sense of humor."

"He's totally in the game of life," I agreed. "I guess he wanted you all to know that he's seeing the reunion happening. He's totally up to date on his parents' lives, no matter where they're traveling!"

After we hung up, I thanked David again for the gift of his unexpectedly sporty metaphor, and took the analogy a little further in my own mind. What I've done with this book is a bit like ESPN highlights; it's a review of the "best of" spiritual exchanges, a montage that captures bits and pieces of the process of spiritual enlightenment.

The stories highlighted in this book are just a small percentage of the exchanges I've had during my career as a medium. There have been profound changes in many lives because of the information I've "caught" over the years. I take no credit for any of it. Any of us can have an intuitive hit, and knock it out of the park. I'm just the catcher: once you step up to home plate, the glory is all yours.

And so, like all experiences in this life, the final chapter of this book unfolded precisely as it should. I give my love to all those who have shared their stories with me—and with you, the reader. We've looked at love from both sides now, and with the help of the many players of Team Life and Team Afterlife, we're emerging more every day.

So stand up, stretch during this Seventh Heaven inning, breathe, and know: all that is, all is one. You are me, and I am you.

See you later!

Alaine

Acknowledgments

Gratitude and acknowledgment goes out to all of those who were directly and indirectly involved with this book project. No matter on which side of the veil you reside, it's been a novel offering! Thank you for allowing me to share your stories. They are guideposts on our common pathway to self-discovery.

Bryna René, thank you for your editorial support, and for being playful and trusting (just like the magical dolphins who brought us together). Thanks as well for building a peaceful dam to stop the overflowing streams of consciousness when necessary!

Thanks to Louise Hay for validating my mind/body intuitions and inspiring my "Issues in the Tissues" theory. I've had the 1984 edition of *You Can Heal Your Life* beside my bed for thirty years. That trust led me to your publishing house, Balboa Press, three generations later. Thanks to the company's team for their handling of this manuscript of metaphysics. "Hay now!"

To the teachers, students, guardians, and conscious community of the Yoga Center of Medford, I offer my eternal gratitude. I'm so grateful for your trust in me, and your willingness to delve deep through yoga, meditation, and channeling sessions. You've shown up, written, hosted, listened, and shared in an exquisite way. Stacey and Diane, you intuitively balance the Center, and wholeheartedly support every soul-seeker who walks through the doors. We're all grateful for Flossie, and her work to spread the word of Yoga during the Center's infancy. Alice, Bo, Bonnie, Ellyn, Joe, Justin, Karin, Kim, Stacy, Sue, Kim, Ted are YCOM's starting line-up, and I'm grateful for your guardianship throughout the years. Accolades are present for Anna's crystal bowl concerts; they became the original soundtrack for many students' meditative journeys.

No words can adequately convey my gratitude to my husband, Keith, for riding the waves of my spiritual projects. Your steadfast support in spiritual messaging, yoga retreats, teaching and traveling and Center Community has supported thousands of recipients, including me. Perpetual patience: you wear it well! Your generous encouragement to write, channel, teach, and share the love are royal rewards.

Nicole, "The Listener." Late at night, early in the morning, story after story, you remained in love with the spiritual communication, and caught every word. No words can describe "us" in "trust."

Slone, "Beaner," my child with a heart of gold, you've proven that my most successful creative project ever was nurturing my children! You had a keen psychic sense even as a toddler, always winning the memory game in minutes. Trust the integrity of your heart and mind. They're both beautiful.

Storm, you were my teacher from birth. When you were a toddler twin, you never left my side. You've found another home in Sierra Leone, and you're still annoyed that it's a poem! Your personal compass points toward worldwide compassion. Be a beacon of light to liberate others from their separation.

Mom, thank you for all of your nurturing. And as you're such an ardent reader, perhaps you'll read my book as well?

Gratitude also goes out to H.A.R.R.P.: Hank, Abraham, Rita, Ronnie, and Paula. Thanks for your Herculean offerings of music and organization. Dearly departed, you've shared the miraculous reality you live in, and have made Heaven feel like my second hometown!

To my soul sisters Judy, Julie, Erica, Maureen, Nancy, and Mary (aka, the Ya-Yas): it took an athletic village to raise our kids, and lots of lemons became delicious lemonade.

Matt, you are a magician. I'm glad our paths crossed in this lifetime and in others, allowing creativity to flourish. C.J., your belief and enthusiasm for sharing lessons of consciousness both professionally and personally is contagious! Kris, thank you for your trust in my dreams: I believe in yours equally. Chris, your home is where your heart is; I'm forever grateful for your open houses. Rosa, I appreciate your unwavering support from Negril, Jamaica. Jade, I'm grateful for our childhood musings of universal wisdom; back then it was called "imagination." Bonnie, your guidance on all matters (and the fact that you compared me to John Edwards early on in my psychic immersion) has been inspiring.

Finally, I offer my deepest gratitude to all of the spirits who trusted me to be a channel for their messages to their beloveds. The earthly shape-shifting for those with whom we've connected has molded me into a humble servant.

The life, the love, the living, it's eternal...

About the Author

Gifted yogi, spiritual teacher, and medium Alaine Portner specializes in delivering message from spirits in the form of life-affirming insights. Her offbeat humor goes straight to the heart, leaving clients with a feeling of connection, support, and lasting love in both this world and the next. Over the last thirty years, her work has made a difference in the lives of thousands across the United States.

Alaine founded the Yoga Center of Medford in Medford, New Jersey, in 1999. Today, the Center houses many gifted teachers and hosts enriching programs in various disciplines. From this spiritual second home, Alaine leads regular guided channeling meditations, and engages her passion to help people discover their personal, physical, and spiritual growth through yoga and meditation. She also leads regional, national, and international events and retreats.

Alaine holds a Bachelor of Science degree in Health Sciences from Temple University, as well as numerous training certifications in physical and spiritual disciplines. When not facilitating at the Center, she can be found cross-training for triathlons, mentoring aspiring yoga teachers, and hanging out with her Ya-Yas. She currently resides in New Jersey with her family of five.

CPSIA information can be obtained at www.ICGtesting.com
Printed in the USA
BVOW03s0421140114

341515BV00006B/4/P